Greetings
IN CROSS-STITCH

The Vanessa-Ann Collection

Oxmoor House®

This friend of ours
    With whom we can
    Laugh, cry, hope, disagree,
    Share the good times,
    Forget the bad.
This friend of ours, Pam.

© 1988 by Oxmoor House, Inc.
Book Division of Southern Progress Corporation
P.O. Box 2463, Birmingham, Alabama 35201

Library of Congress Catalog Number: 86-62286
ISBN: 0-8487-0700-1
Manufactured in the United States of America
Second Printing 1990

Executive Editor: Candace N. Conard
Production Manager: Jerry Higdon
Associate Production Manager: Rick Litton
Art Director: Bob Nance

Greetings in Cross-Stitch

Editor: Linda Baltzell Wright
Assistant Editor: Kim Eidson Crane
Editorial Assistant: Karolyn Morgan
Copy Chief: Mary Jean Haddin
Designer: Diana Smith Morrison
Photographers: Ryne Hazen, Colleen Duffley

Much of the photography in this book was done on location at Trends and Traditions, part of Historic 25th Street in Ogden, Utah. The Vanessa-Ann Collection expresses its thanks to Mary Gaskill for her cooperation.

To find out how you can order *Cooking Light* magazine, write to *Cooking Light*®, P.O. Box C-549, Birmingham, AL 35283

Contents

Introduction............ 4

Special Occasions

NEW BABY

Little bunny.................................6
Congratulations.......................8

ANNIVERSARY

The holiest of holidays............ 10
Happy anniversary................... 12

THANK YOU

School-days heart.....................14
Thank you................................ 16

GET WELL

Get well....................................17
Hope you're feeling
   better soon..........................18

HAPPY BIRTHDAY

Birthday clowns....................... 20
Happy sweet sixteen................ 24
Birthday cheers!....................... 26
Over the hill............................. 28
Happy birthday........................ 30
You're #1!.................................32
A little something for you........ 34

Celebrations

Happy graduation!.................... 36
Eat, drink, and remarry.......... 38
Applause! Applause!................. 40
Cheers!.....................................42

Friendship

Thanks for popping
   into my life...........................48
You are the apple of my eye... 50
A basketful of love.................... 51
A friend is a neighbor
   of the heart...........................52
I go to pieces without you.......54
Let me give you a hand...........60

Just Because

Keep smiling!............................ 62
Life is like a rosebud...............64
Violets bloom........................... 66
To create a little flower...........68
Starlight, starbright..................70

Love

Please write............................. 72
It's unbearable without you..... 74
I love you.................................77
Udderly in love........................ 80

Home, Sweet Home

Welcome to my roost...............84
For your new home................. 88
Home, sweet home...................90
Places in my heart...................92
Mooove it!.................................94

Sympathy

With deepest sympathy............ 98
Where is the heart.................. 100
Our cares behind................... 102

Holidays

VALENTINE'S DAY

I love you................................104
Be mine.................................. 106

EASTER

He is risen!............................. 108
Happy Easter.......................... 110

MOTHER'S DAY

A mother understands............ 114
I love you with all
   of my hearts...................... 117

FATHER'S DAY

Happy Father's Day.................118

GRANDPARENTS' DAY

The sands of gold....................120

CHRISTMAS

The heart of Christmas.......... 122
Christmas peace......................124
In the udder confusion...........127
Twelve days of Christmas.......130

General Instructions........... 139

Suppliers 143

More than the gift is the greeting, or at least that's how we feel at The Vanessa-Ann Collection. So we have filled these pages with heartfelt greetings for all occasions. There are birthday proclamations, romantic notes, messages of congratulation, farewell wishes, holiday greetings, and words of consolation. These delightfully simple projects reflect a potpourri of ideas you will want to stitch for the people who mean the most to you. Made with your hands and your time, these cards state . . . it's from the heart!

Special Occasions

A little bunny with a heart of blue
Carries good wishes to baby and you!

SAMPLE

Stitched on white Aida 18, the finished design size is 7/8" x 1 1/8". (Adjust project measurements for other stitch counts.) The fabric was cut 6" x 6".

MATERIALS FOR CARD

Completed cross-stitch; white thread
1/2 yard of 1/8"-wide blue satin ribbon
1/2 yard of 1/16"-wide blue rayon braid; matching thread
Fusible web
Six small white beads
One 4 1/4" x 7" piece of white poster board
One 4 1/4" x 7" piece of blue watercolor paper
Rubber cement
White glue
Tracing paper

DIRECTIONS

1. Trace and cut out the pattern for the heart. Fold the blue paper in half to make a 4 1/4" x 3 1/2" card. Center and trace the heart pattern onto the front of the blue paper. Cut out the heart. Stitch 1/8" to 1/4" outside the heart window, using white thread and a medium stitch.

2. Cut the Aida 3 1/4" x 2 3/4", with the design centered. Cut the fusible web 3 1/4" x 2 3/4".

3. Fold the poster board in half to make a 4 1/4" x 3 1/2" card. Center and fuse the stitched Aida to the front of the card, according to manufacturer's directions. Place the white card inside the blue paper so that the stitched design is centered in the window. Rubber-cement the outside edges of the blue paper to the front of the white card.

4. Cut the satin ribbon into two 3 1/2" lengths and two 4 1/4" lengths. Glue the ribbon to the edges of the card, overlapping the ends at the corners.

5. Fold the rayon braid into 2" loops and knot the loops to form a bow. Attach the bow with white glue or thread to the front of the card (see photo).

6. Glue the beads to the front of the card (see photo).

Heart Pattern

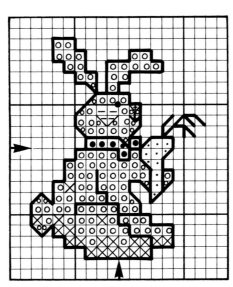

Stitch Count: 16 x 20

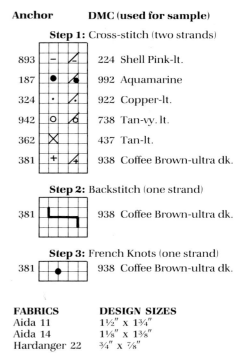

Anchor			DMC (used for sample)
Step 1: Cross-stitch (two strands)			
893	–	╱	224 Shell Pink-lt.
187	●	╱	992 Aquamarine
324	·	╱	922 Copper-lt.
942	O	╱	738 Tan-vy. lt.
362	✕		437 Tan-lt.
381	+	╱	938 Coffee Brown-ultra dk.

Step 2: Backstitch (one strand)

381	└	938 Coffee Brown-ultra dk.

Step 3: French Knots (one strand)

381	●	938 Coffee Brown-ultra dk.

FABRICS	DESIGN SIZES
Aida 11	1 1/2" x 1 3/4"
Aida 14	1 1/8" x 1 3/8"
Hardanger 22	3/4" x 7/8"

Stitch Count: 53 x 25

Congratulations on the new arrival!

SAMPLE

Stitched on white Aida 18 over two threads, the finished design size is 3″ x 1⅜″. (Adjust project measurements for other stitch counts.) The fabric was cut 8″ x 9″.

MATERIALS FOR PILLOW

Completed cross-stitch
⅝ yard of 45″-wide blue pindot fabric; matching thread
1¼ yards of 1/16″-wide blue rayon braid; matching thread
2 yards of ⅛″-wide white satin ribbon; matching thread
Stuffing
Dressmakers' pen
Tracing paper

Anchor		DMC (used for sample)

Step 1: Cross-stitch (two strands)

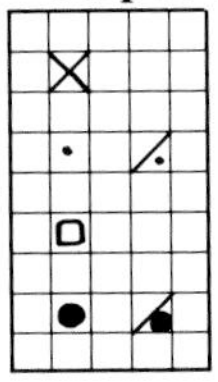

117	X	341	Blue Violet-lt.
168	· /	807	Peacock Blue
214	▢	966	Baby Green-med.
875	● ◢	503	Blue Green-med.

Step 2: Backstitch (one strand)

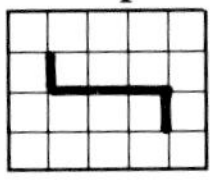

| 401 | | 844 | Beaver Gray-ultra dk. |

Step 3: French Knots (one strand)

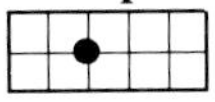

| 401 | ● | 844 | Beaver Gray-ultra dk. |

FABRICS	DESIGN SIZES
Aida 11	4¾″ x 2¼″
Aida 14	3¾″ x 1¾″
Hardanger 22	2⅜″ x 1⅛″

DIRECTIONS

All seam allowances are ¼″.

1. Cut the Aida 6″ x 6″, with the design centered.

2. Cut two 8″ x 6½″ pieces from the pindot fabric. Also cut a 3½″-wide bias strip, piecing as needed to equal 66″.

3. Trace and cut out the window pattern. Center the pattern over one piece of pindot fabric. Trace around the pattern.

4. Cut the pindot fabric ¼″ inside the pen line. Clip the seam allowances and fold under. Center and pin the stitched design behind the opening. Slipstitch the edges of the opening to the design.

5. Cut one 18″ length from the blue rayon braid. Leave 2″ of the braid ends loose at the center bottom, and slipstitch the braid to the pillow front, ¼″ outside the Aida. With the remaining braid, form five 1½″ loops. Tie the 2″ ends around the center of the loops.

6. With right sides together, stitch the ends of the bias strip to form one continuous strip. Fold the bias strip in half lengthwise, with wrong sides together, so that it measures 1¾″ wide; then press. Machine-stitch the white ribbon to the bias strip through both layers, ¼″ from the fold.

7. Using the dressmakers' pen, mark the center of each edge of the pillow front. Divide the bias strip into quarters; mark the quarters on the raw edge.

8. Stitch gathering threads through both layers of the bias strip, next to the raw edge. Gather the strip to make a ruffle. Match the marks on the ruffle to the marks on the edges of the pillow front. Pin the ruffle to the pillow front, aligning the raw edges and easing in fullness at the corners. Stitch through all layers.

9. With the ruffle toward the center of the pillow, pin the right sides of the pillow front and back together. Stitch on the stitching line of the ruffle, leaving a 3″ opening for turning. Turn the pillow right side out and stuff. Slipstitch the opening closed.

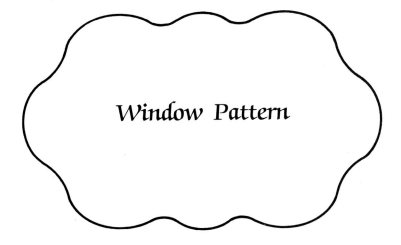

Window Pattern

The holiest of all holidays
Are those kept by ourselves
In silence and apart:
The secret holidays of the heart.

SAMPLE

Stitched on Glenshee Egyptian Cotton quality D over two threads, the finished design size is 8⅛" x 10¼". (Adjust project measurements for other stitch counts.) The fabric was cut 15" x 17".

MATERIALS FOR MAT

Completed cross-stitch
Professionally cut mat
Glue
Masking tape
Pencil or chalk
Dressmakers' pen

DIRECTIONS

1. Have a professional framer cut the mat board 10¼" x 12" and the window 3¾" x 5⅝" for a 4" x 6" photograph.

2. Place the stitched design wrong side up on a flat surface. Center the mat on the stitched design so that the fabric will extend at least 1½" beyond the mat on all sides. Trace the window of the mat on the design piece. Draw another line 1½" inside the window. Cut the fabric along the inside line. Clip corners to the first line at a 45° angle.

3. Center the mat on the wrong side of the design, aligning it with the pencil lines on the fabric. Run a line of glue along the top inside edge of the mat. Fold the fabric over the mat and tape it at two or three points. Repeat for the bottom inside edge, then sides.

4. Run a line of glue along the top outside edge of the mat to within 2" of the corners. Fold the fabric over the edge, pulling the surface taut. Tape. Repeat along the bottom edge, then sides.

5. Place glue at each corner and fold the fabric over it, securing it with tape. Let the glue dry overnight. Remove the tape. Insert the mat into a purchased frame.

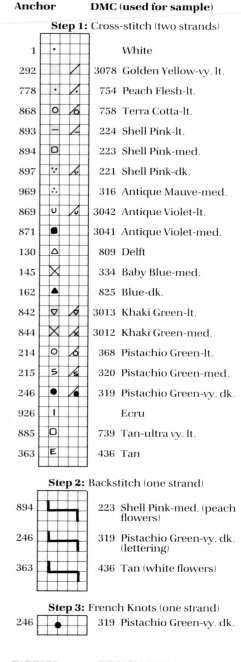

Anchor			DMC (used for sample)	
Step 1: Cross-stitch (two strands)				
1	•			White
292		/	3078	Golden Yellow-vy. lt.
778	•	/	754	Peach Flesh-lt.
868	O	6	758	Terra Cotta-lt.
893	−	/	224	Shell Pink-lt.
894	□		223	Shell Pink-med.
897	∵	/	221	Shell Pink-dk.
969	∴		316	Antique Mauve-med.
869	U	6	3042	Antique Violet-lt.
871	■		3041	Antique Violet-med.
130	△		809	Delft
145	X		334	Baby Blue-med.
162	▲		825	Blue-dk.
842	▽	6	3013	Khaki Green-lt.
844	X	/	3012	Khaki Green-med.
214	O	6	368	Pistachio Green-lt.
215	S	6	320	Pistachio Green-med.
246	●	6	319	Pistachio Green-vy. dk.
926	I			Ecru
885	□		739	Tan-ultra vy. lt.
363	E		436	Tan

Anchor			DMC (used for sample)	
Step 2: Backstitch (one strand)				
894	⌐		223	Shell Pink-med. (peach flowers)
246	⌐		319	Pistachio Green-vy. dk. (lettering)
363	⌐		436	Tan (white flowers)

Anchor			DMC (used for sample)	
Step 3: French Knots (one strand)				
246	●		319	Pistachio Green-vy. dk.

FABRICS	DESIGN SIZES
Aida 11	9⅝" x 12⅛"
Aida 14	7⅝" x 9⅝"
Aida 18	5⅞" x 7½"
Hardanger 22	4⅞" x 6⅛"

Stitch Count: 106 x 134

Happy Anniversary

SAMPLE

Stitched on white Belfast Linen 32 over two threads, the finished design size of the largest numeral is 1⅝″ x 1¾″. (Adjust project measurements for other stitch counts.) Fabric was cut 8″ x 6″ for each.

MATERIALS FOR ONE TAG

Completed cross-stitch; matching thread
One 5½″ x 3½″ piece of unstitched white Belfast Linen 32
½ yard of ¼″-wide white flat lace
½ yard of ¾″-wide ecru flat lace
68 gold beads for "25" or 20 gold beads for "50"
⅜ yard of ⅛″-wide white satin ribbon
One small piece of polyester fleece

DIRECTIONS

All seam allowances are ¼″.

1. Cut the linen 5½″ x 3½″, with the design centered. Cut one piece of fleece 5½″ x 3½″.

2. Center and pin the fleece to the wrong side of design. Baste. Cut the ecru lace into two 6″ lengths and two 4″ lengths. Fold the ends under ¼″. With the finished edge of the lace toward the center of the design, pin the lace to the right side of the design. Baste along seam lines.

3. With right sides together, pin design piece to back piece and stitch, leaving a 2″ opening. Trim fleece from the seam allowance. Clip corners and turn. Slipstitch the opening closed.

4. On the "25" design piece, slipstitch the white lace ¼″ inside the front edge. Sew the gold beads under the design, directly above the lace. On "50," slipstitch the white lace ⅛″ from the edge, with the lace extending beyond the piece. Sew five gold beads ⅛″ inside the edge of the lace at each corner (see photo).

5. Knot the ribbon ends. Tack the knots to the front upper corners.

Anchor	DMC (used for sample)

Step 1: Cross-stitch (one strand)

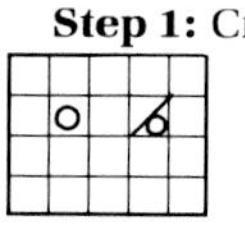

Gold Metallic ("50") or Silver Metallic ("25")

Step 2: Backstitch (one strand)

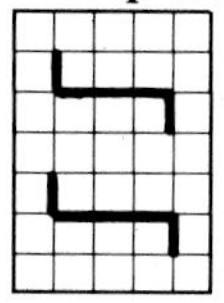

400   317 Pewter Gray (outline of numerals in "25")

Gold Metallic (all else)

FABRICS	DESIGN SIZES
Aida 11	2⅜″ x 2½″
Aida 14	1⅞″ x 1⅞″
Aida 18	1½″ x 1½″
Hardanger 22	1⅛″ x 1¼″

Stitch Count (for one number): 26 x 27

Stitched on cream Aida 18, the finished design size is 3⅞" x 2⅝". (Adjust project measurements for other stitch counts.) The fabric was cut 7" x 6".

MATERIALS FOR CARD

Completed cross-stitch
Fusible web
One 7¼" x 9" piece of cream
   watercolor paper
One 7¼" x 4¼" piece of cream
   watercolor paper
One 6½" x 8" piece of yellow
   paper
One 8" x 5" piece of textured
   green wrapping paper;
   matching thread
Two paper heart stickers: one
   yellow, one orange
Rubber cement
Tracing paper

DIRECTIONS

1. For the front of the card, fold the wrapping paper around the 7¼" x 4¼" piece of watercolor paper, creasing the folds. Glue the edges of the wrapping paper to the back of the watercolor paper.

2. Trace and cut out the heart pattern. Trace the heart onto the back of the covered paper, placing the heart off-center. Cut out the heart to make a window.

3. Center the stitched design behind the window. To attach the design, stitch ⅛" outside the window, using green thread and a medium stitch. Trim the Aida ½" outside the stitching.

What a year ~
Filled with fun.
Thanks to you ~
You're #1!

Heart Pattern

Stitch Count: 71 x 50

4. Score the remaining piece of watercolor paper in the center to make a 7¼″ x 4½″ folded card.

5. Cut one 7¼″ x 4¼″ piece of fusible web. Following manufacturer's instructions, fuse the back of the Aida to the folded watercolor paper, allowing ¼″ of the card to extend below the green paper. Machine-stitch along the top edge of the green paper through all layers, using green thread and a medium stitch.

6. Place two heart stickers on the upper left side of the card.

7. Fold the yellow paper to measure 6½″ x 4″. Place it inside the card, matching the fold line to the score line of the card. Attach the paper with rubber cement along the score line.

Anchor		DMC (used for sample)
Step 1:		Cross-stitch (two strands)
1		White
306	– ⁄	725 Topaz
324	O ⁄	721 Orange Spice-med.
11	I ⁄	350 Coral-med.
19	● ⁄	817 Coral Red-vy. dk.
160	▫	813 Blue-lt.
161	△ ⁄	826 Blue-med.
244	✕ ⁄	987 Forest Green-dk.
349	■ ⁄	301 Mahogany-med.

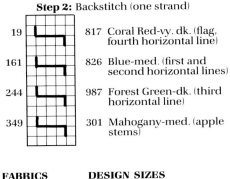

Step 2: Backstitch (one strand)

19		817 Coral Red-vy. dk. (flag, fourth horizontal line)
161		826 Blue-med. (first and second horizontal lines)
244		987 Forest Green-dk. (third horizontal line)
349		301 Mahogany-med. (apple stems)

FABRICS	DESIGN SIZES
Aida 11	6½″ x 4½″
Aida 14	5⅛″ x 3⅝″
Hardanger 22	3¼″ x 2¼″

Thank You **15**

A little bag of treats
Because you are so sweet!

SAMPLE

Stitched on a ready-made tote bag, using Waste Canvas 14, the finished design size is 3⅝" x 1⅝". (Adjust project measurements for other stitch counts.) The waste canvas was cut 6" x 4". See Materials and Directions to make your own bags or refer to Suppliers for information on ordering bags.

MATERIALS FOR TOTE

One 6" x 13" piece of cream
  canvas; matching thread
½ yard of 1"-wide cream
  webbing
1 yard of ⅛"-wide dark blue
  ribbon
1 yard of ⅛"-wide light blue
  ribbon

DIRECTIONS

All seam allowances are ¼".

1. Along one 13" edge of the canvas, press ¼" to the wrong side.

Anchor	DMC (used for sample)
Step 1: Backstitch (one strand)	
164	824 Blue-vy. dk.

FABRICS	DESIGN SIZES
Aida 11	3⅛" x 2⅞"
Aida 14	2⅜" x 2¼"
Aida 18	1⅞" x 1¾"
Hardanger 22	1½" x 1⅜"

2. Cut the webbing into two equal lengths. Pin the raw ends to the wrong side of the canvas on the folded edge (Diagram A), making sure handles will align when bag is finished. Stitch ⅛" from the fold, catching the ends of the webbing.

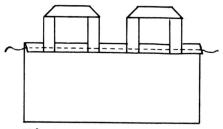

Diagram A

3. Fold the canvas with right sides together so that it measures 5¾" x 6½". Stitch down the side and across the bottom edge, backstitching at the beginning and end.

4. With the tote still inside out, align the side and bottom seams, forming a corner. Stitch across the corner (Diagram B). Form another corner on the opposite side of the tote and stitch. Trim both corners. Turn tote right side out, and it's ready for cross-stitching.

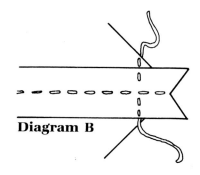

Diagram B

5. Handling all the ribbons as one unit, tie a bow around one end of the tote handle.

Stitch Count: 34 x 31

Here's to a speedy recovery!

SAMPLE

Stitched on a ready-made tote bag, using Waste Canvas 14, the finished design size is 4½″ x 3⅜″. (Adjust project measurements for other stitch counts.) The waste canvas was cut 5″ x 5″. See Materials and Directions to make your own bags or refer to Suppliers for information on ordering bags.

MATERIALS FOR TOTE

One 6″ x 13″ piece of cream canvas; matching thread
½ yard of 1″-wide cream webbing

DIRECTIONS

Complete Steps 1–4 of the thank you tote, page 16.

Anchor		DMC (used for sample)
Step 1: Cross-stitch (two strands)		
8	•	353 Peach Flesh
10	✕	352 Coral-lt.
11	●	350 Coral-med.
5975	O	356 Terra Cotta-med.
215	−	320 Pistachio Green-med.
Step 2: Backstitch (one strand)		
5975		356 Terra Cotta-med. (flowers)
246		319 Pistachio Green-vy. dk. (leaves)

FABRICS	DESIGN SIZES
Aida 11	5⅝″ x 4¼″
Aida 14	4½″ x 3⅜″
Aida 18	3½″ x 2⅝″
Hardanger 22	2⅞″ x 2⅛″

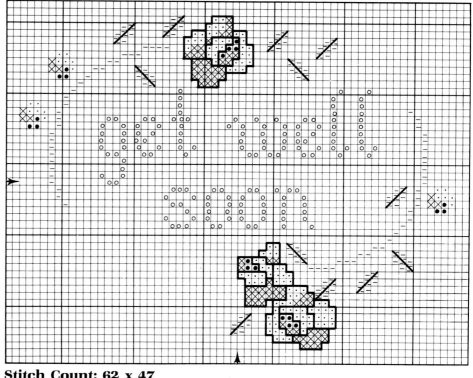

Stitch Count: 62 x 47

Hope you're feeling better soon.

SAMPLE

Stitched on white Belfast Linen 32 over two threads, the finished design size is 2" x 2⅛". (Adjust project measurements for other stitch counts.) The fabric was cut 17" x 21". Position the stitched design so that its center is 7" from the left 21" edge of the fabric and 3½" from the bottom 17" edge.

Stitch Count: 33 x 34

Anchor		DMC (used for sample)
Step 1: Cross-stitch (two strands)		
386	−	746 Off White
300	∴	745 Yellow-lt. pale
49	·	3689 Mauve-lt.
108	O	211 Lavender-lt.
104	X	210 Lavender-med.
105	▲	209 Lavender-dk.
215	■	368 Pistachio Green-lt.
887	●	3046 Yellow Beige-med.

Step 2: Backstitch (one strand)

110		208 Lavender-vy. dk.

Step 3: French Knots (one strand)

373	●	3045 Yellow Beige-dk.

Step 4: Long Stitch (one strand)

373	╲	3045 Yellow Beige-dk. (stamens)

FABRICS	DESIGN SIZES
Aida 11	3" x 3⅛"
Aida 14	2⅜" x 2⅜"
Aida 18	1⅞" x 1⅞"
Hardanger 22	1½" x 1½"

MATERIALS FOR ENVELOPE

Completed cross-stitch
One 14″ x 14″ piece of mauve
   fabric
1½ yards of ½″-wide tan rayon
   seam binding; matching
   thread
Fusible web
Three ⅜″ lavender buttons
Dressmakers' pen

DIRECTIONS

1. Make a paper pattern and practice the folds before cutting the linen. Mark the fold lines and cutting lines on the linen with the dressmakers' pen. Cut carefully.

2. Use the dressmakers' pen to mark the envelope pattern on the linen (Diagram A). The bottom of the design is ¾″ from the bottom left corner of fabric. Note position of the straight of grain of the fabric. Fuse the design piece to the lining, according to manufacturer's directions. Cut on pen lines.

3. Fold the rayon binding in half and press. Encase the edges of the linen in the binding. Machine-stitch through all layers, folding the corners of the binding at a 45° angle.

4. Fold the linen piece as shown in Diagrams B through G. Press.

5. Sew the buttons on the front of the envelope (see photo).

6. Slipstitch the edges on the front of the envelope together, leaving the top end open.

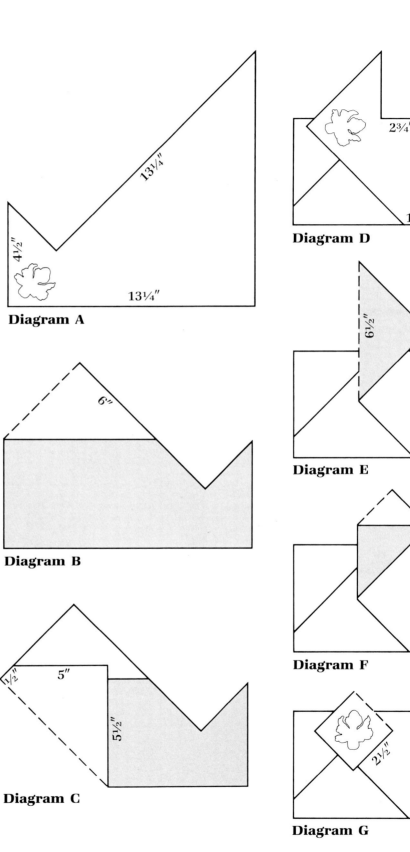

Diagram A

Diagram B

Diagram C

Diagram D

Diagram E

Diagram F

Diagram G

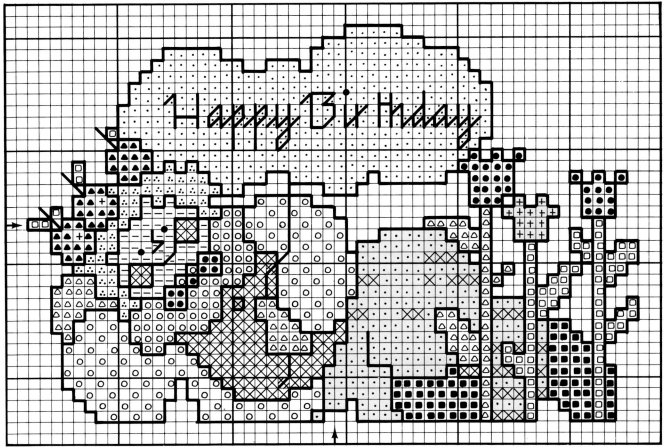

Stitch Count: 54 x 35

It's your day to clown around! Happy Birthday!

SAMPLES

Happy Birthday Clown: Stitched on white Perforated Paper 15, the finished design size is 3⅝″ x 2⅜″. (Adjust project measurements for other stitch counts.) The paper was cut 6″ x 6″.

Clown Standing on His Head: Stitched on white Perforated Paper 15, the finished design size is 3⅜″ x 3¾″. (Adjust project measurements for other stitch counts.) Paper was cut 6″ x 6″.

Clown on Roller Skates: Stitched on white Perforated Paper 15, the finished design size is 1¾″ x 4⅛″. (Adjust project measurements for other stitch counts.) The paper was cut 6″ x 6″.

Anchor		DMC (used for sample)
		Step 1: Cross-stitch (three strands)
1	−	White
303	∴	742 Tangerine-lt.
881	•	945 Sportsman Flesh
10	+	352 Coral-lt.
27	X	899 Rose-med.
42	▲	309 Rose-deep
99	●	552 Violet-dk.
168	O	518 Wedgewood-lt.
978	•	322 Navy Blue-vy. lt.
147	X	312 Navy Blue-lt.
265	△	3348 Yellow Green-lt.
205	◻	911 Emerald Green-med.
309	■	435 Brown-vy. lt.

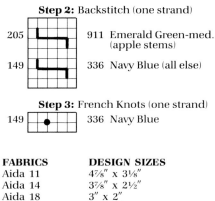

Step 2: Backstitch (one strand)

205		911 Emerald Green-med. (apple stems)
149		336 Navy Blue (all else)

Step 3: French Knots (one strand)

| 149 | ● | 336 Navy Blue |

FABRICS	DESIGN SIZES
Aida 11	4⅞″ x 3⅛″
Aida 14	3⅞″ x 2½″
Aida 18	3″ x 2″
Hardanger 22	2½″ x 1⅝″

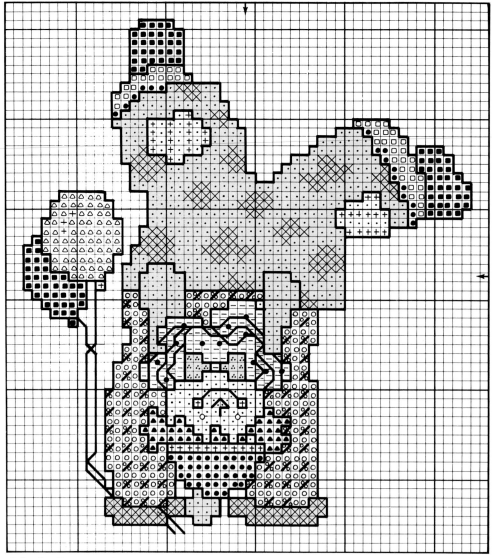

Stitch Count: 50 x 57

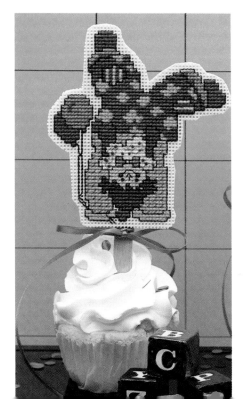

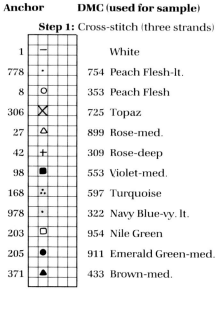

Anchor		DMC (used for sample)
Step 1: Cross-stitch (three strands)		
1	−	White
778	·	754 Peach Flesh-lt.
8	○	353 Peach Flesh
306	✕	725 Topaz
27	△	899 Rose-med.
42	+	309 Rose-deep
98	■	553 Violet-med.
168	∴	597 Turquoise
978	·	322 Navy Blue-vy. lt.
203	□	954 Nile Green
205	●	911 Emerald Green-med.
371	▲	433 Brown-med.

Step 2: Backstitch (one strand)

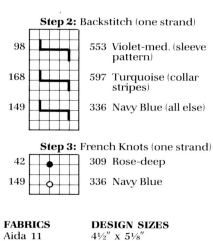

98	553 Violet-med. (sleeve pattern)
168	597 Turquoise (collar stripes)
149	336 Navy Blue (all else)

Step 3: French Knots (one strand)

| 42 | ● | 309 Rose-deep |
| 149 | ○ | 336 Navy Blue |

FABRICS | **DESIGN SIZES**
Aida 11 | 4½″ x 5⅛″
Aida 14 | 3⅝″ x 4⅛″
Aida 18 | 2¾″ x 3⅛″
Hardanger 22 | 2¼″ x 2⅝″

MATERIALS FOR CLOWNS

Completed cross-stitch
1½ yards of ⅛″-wide purple satin ribbon
Three 4″ x 5″ pieces of medium-weight white paper
Three popsicle sticks
Rubber cement
Craft knife with sharp blade

DIRECTIONS

1. Glue each stitched clown to a piece of white paper. Following the general shape of the clown, cut through both layers of paper, at least one hole outside the design (see photo).

2. Glue a popsicle stick to the back of each clown, with 2½″ to 3″ of the stick extending below the design piece.

3. Cut the ribbon into three 18″ lengths. Tie a bow around each stick below the design.

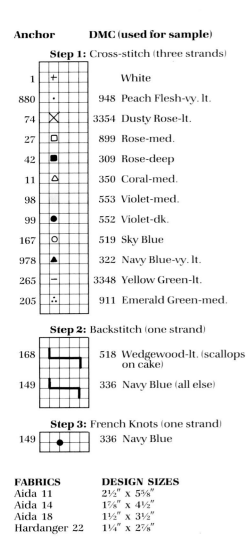

Anchor		DMC (used for sample)
Step 1: Cross-stitch (three strands)		
1	+	White
880	·	948 Peach Flesh-vy. lt.
74	X	3354 Dusty Rose-lt.
27	□	899 Rose-med.
42	■	309 Rose-deep
11	△	350 Coral-med.
98		553 Violet-med.
99	●	552 Violet-dk.
167	O	519 Sky Blue
978	▲	322 Navy Blue-vy. lt.
265	−	3348 Yellow Green-lt.
205	∴	911 Emerald Green-med.
Step 2: Backstitch (one strand)		
168		518 Wedgewood-lt. (scallops on cake)
149		336 Navy Blue (all else)
Step 3: French Knots (one strand)		
149	●	336 Navy Blue

FABRICS	DESIGN SIZES
Aida 11	2½″ x 5⅝″
Aida 14	1⅞″ x 4½″
Aida 18	1½″ x 3½″
Hardanger 22	1¼″ x 2⅞″

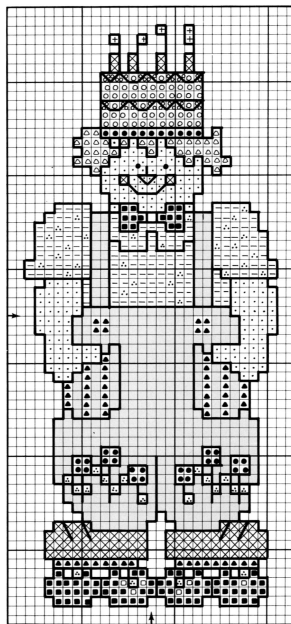

Stitch Count: 27 x 62

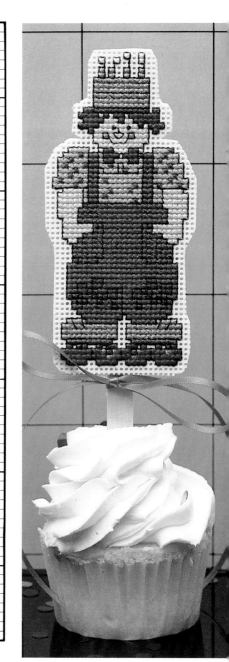

Happy Sweet Sixteen

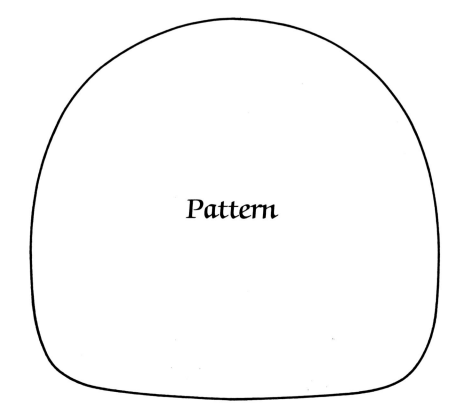

Pattern

SAMPLE

Stitched on white Belfast Linen 32 over two threads, the finished design size is 3½" x 3¼". (Adjust project measurements for other stitch counts.) The fabric was cut 7" x 6".

MATERIALS FOR CARD

Completed cross-stitch
1 yard each of the following ribbons: ⅛"-wide lavender satin, ¹⁄₁₆"-wide white satin, ¹⁄₁₆"-wide green rayon braid, ¹⁄₁₆"-wide tan rayon braid
One 9" square of medium-weight blue paper
One 5" square of white poster board
Fusible web
White glue
Tracing paper

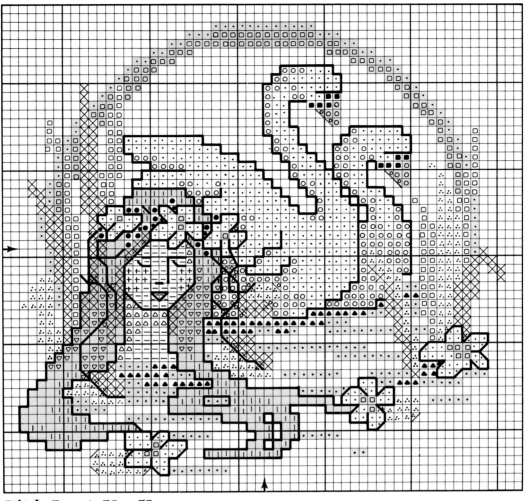

Stitch Count: 56 x 52

DIRECTIONS

1. Trace and cut out the pattern. Trace the pattern onto the poster board and the fusible web; cut out.

2. Score the blue paper in the center to make a 4½" x 9" card.

3. Center the fusible web and poster board behind the stitched design and fuse together. Trim the fabric ½" outside the edges of the poster board and clip the curved edges. Fold the fabric to the back of the poster board and glue. Then glue the design piece to the front of the medium-weight blue paper card, placing the left edge of the design ¾" from the left edge of the card.

4. Handling all the ribbons as one unit, wrap them around the left side of the card and tie a knot (see photo). Trim the ends to irregular lengths.

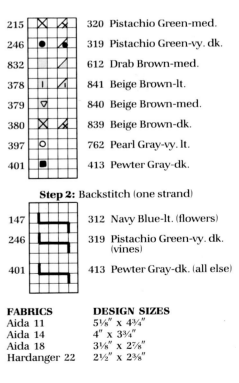

Anchor			DMC (used for sample)

Step 1: Cross-stitch (two strands)

1	·	╱	White
366	−	╱	951 Sportsman Flesh-vy. lt.
4146	△	◿	950 Sportsman Flesh-lt.
778	+	╱	754 Peach Flesh-lt.
300	▢		745 Yellow-lt. pale
891	◑	◢	676 Old Gold-lt.
167	·	╱	519 Sky Blue
168	▲	◣	518 Wedgewood-lt.
214	∴	╱	368 Pistachio Green-lt.
216	▢		367 Pistachio Green-dk.
215	☒	◺	320 Pistachio Green-med.
246	●	◖	319 Pistachio Green-vy. dk.
832		╱	612 Drab Brown-med.
378	∣	╱	841 Beige Brown-lt.
379	▽		840 Beige Brown-med.
380	☒	◪	839 Beige Brown-dk.
397	○		762 Pearl Gray-vy. lt.
401	■		413 Pewter Gray-dk.

Step 2: Backstitch (one strand)

147		312 Navy Blue-lt. (flowers)
246		319 Pistachio Green-vy. dk. (vines)
401		413 Pewter Gray-dk. (all else)

FABRICS	DESIGN SIZES
Aida 11	5⅛" x 4¾"
Aida 14	4" x 3¾"
Aida 18	3⅛" x 2⅞"
Hardanger 22	2½" x 2⅜"

BIRThDAY cheers!

SAMPLE

Stitched on cream Aida 18, the finished design size is 4″ x 4¾″. (Adjust project measurements for other stitch counts.) The fabric was cut 14″ x 9″.

MATERIALS FOR LABEL

Completed cross-stitch
One 12½″ x 6″ piece of cream fabric; matching thread
1¼ yards of ⅛″-wide cream grosgrain ribbon
Eleven dozen gold beads

DIRECTIONS

All seam allowances are ¼″.

1. Cut the Aida 12½″ x 6″, with the design centered horizontally.

2. Pin Aida to cream fabric, right sides together and raw edges aligned. Stitch. Leave 3″ opening for turning. Clip corners. Turn right side out; slipstitch closed.

3. Sew beads along lower edge of Aida, beginning and ending 1½″ from both sides of stitched design.

4. Cut the ribbon into two equal lengths. Center and pin one ribbon length along the top edge of the Aida. (The ribbon will extend 5″ on both sides of the Aida.) Slipstitch the ribbon in place, beginning and ending 2″ from each end of the fabric. Repeat with the second ribbon length, placing it between the design and the beads.

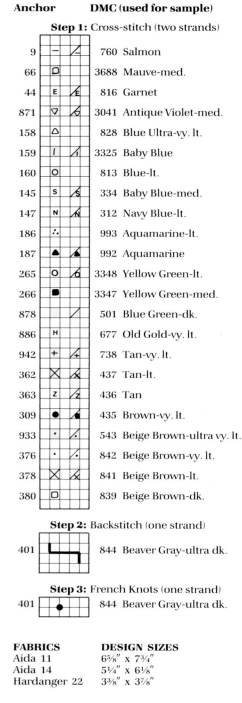

Anchor			DMC (used for sample)	
Step 1: Cross-stitch (two strands)				
9	–	╱	760	Salmon
66	▢		3688	Mauve-med.
44	E	╱E	816	Garnet
871	▽	╱	3041	Antique Violet-med.
158	△		828	Blue Ultra-vy. lt.
159	I	╱	3325	Baby Blue
160	O		813	Blue-lt.
145	S	╱S	334	Baby Blue-med.
147	N	╱N	312	Navy Blue-lt.
186	∴		993	Aquamarine-lt.
187	▲	╱	992	Aquamarine
265	O	╱	3348	Yellow Green-lt.
266	■		3347	Yellow Green-med.
878			501	Blue Green-dk.
886	H		677	Old Gold-vy. lt.
942	+	╱+	738	Tan-vy. lt.
362	✕	╱	437	Tan-lt.
363	Z	╱Z	436	Tan
309	●	╱	435	Brown-vy. lt.
933	·	╱	543	Beige Brown-ultra vy. lt.
376	·	╱	842	Beige Brown-vy. lt.
378	✕	╱	841	Beige Brown-lt.
380	▢		839	Beige Brown-dk.
Step 2: Backstitch (one strand)				
401			844	Beaver Gray-ultra dk.
Step 3: French Knots (one strand)				
401	●		844	Beaver Gray-ultra dk.

FABRICS	DESIGN SIZES
Aida 11	6⅝″ x 7¾″
Aida 14	5¼″ x 6⅛″
Hardanger 22	3⅜″ x 3⅞″

Stitch Count: 73 x 85

Lordy! Lordy! Look who's 40!

SAMPLE

Stitched on black Aida 18, the finished design size is 3″ x 2⅛″. (Adjust project measurements for other stitch counts.) The fabric was cut 8″ x 12″. Substitute numerals in the border as desired.

MATERIALS FOR ENVELOPE

Completed cross-stitch; matching thread
One 5″ x 10¼″ piece of black fabric

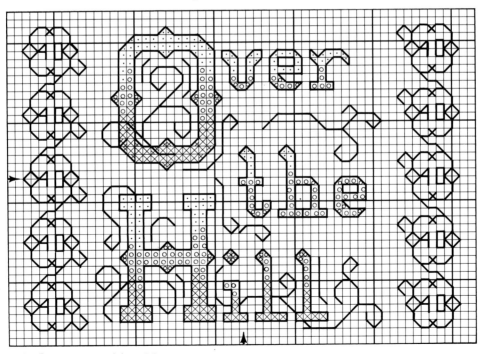

DIRECTIONS

All seam allowances are ¼″.

1. Trim the design piece to 5″ x 10¼″, with the design centered 3½″ from one 5″ edge.

2. Pin the lining to the Aida, right sides together and raw edges aligned. Stitch, leaving a small opening for turning. Clip the corners. Turn right side out and slip-stitch the opening closed.

3. To form a pocket, fold the Aida to the back, ⅞″ below the bottom edge of the design, lining sides together; pin. Topstitch along the sides and across the end of the flap. Fold the flap down to make an envelope.

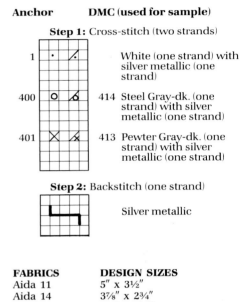

Anchor		DMC (used for sample)

Step 1: Cross-stitch (two strands)

1		White (one strand) with silver metallic (one strand)
400	414	Steel Gray-dk. (one strand) with silver metallic (one strand)
401	413	Pewter Gray-dk. (one strand) with silver metallic (one strand)

Step 2: Backstitch (one strand)

Silver metallic

FABRICS	DESIGN SIZES
Aida 11	5″ x 3½″
Aida 14	3⅞″ x 2¾″
Hardanger 22	2½″ x 1¾″

Stitch Count: 55 x 38

Happy Birthday

SAMPLE

Stitched on white Linda 27 over two threads, the finished design size is 4⅞" x 6½". (Adjust project measurements for other stitch counts.) Fabric was cut 9" x 11".

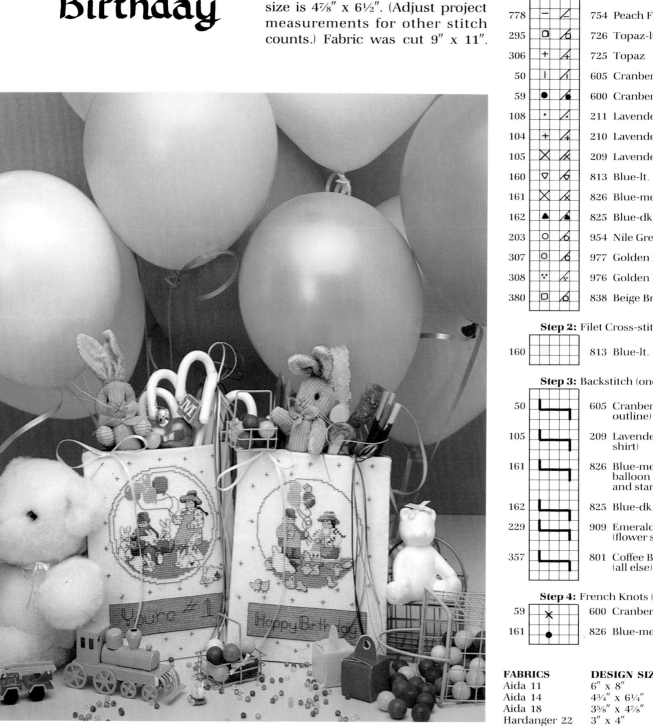

Anchor			DMC (used for sample)
Step 1: Cross-stitch (two strands)			
1	·	/	White
778	–	/	754 Peach Flesh-lt.
295	◨	◹	726 Topaz-lt.
306	+	◿	725 Topaz
50			/	605 Cranberry-vy. lt.
59	●	◢	600 Cranberry-vy. dk.
108	·	/	211 Lavender-lt.
104	+	◿	210 Lavender-med.
105	✕	◿	209 Lavender-dk.
160	▽	◿	813 Blue-lt.
161	✕	◿	826 Blue-med.
162	▲	◢	825 Blue-dk.
203	○	◿	954 Nile Green
307	○	◿	977 Golden Brown-lt.
308	∴	/	976 Golden Brown-med.
380	◨	◿	838 Beige Brown-vy. dk.

Step 2: Filet Cross-stitch (one strand)

160		813 Blue-lt.

Step 3: Backstitch (one strand)

50		605 Cranberry-vy. lt. (dress outline)
105		209 Lavender-dk. (boy's shirt)
161		826 Blue-med. (chicken, balloon strings, circle and stars)
162		825 Blue-dk. (lettering)
229		909 Emerald Green-vy. dk. (flower stems)
357		801 Coffee Brown-dk. (all else)

Step 4: French Knots (one strand)

59	✳	600 Cranberry-vy. dk.
161	●	826 Blue-med.

FABRICS	DESIGN SIZES
Aida 11	6" x 8"
Aida 14	4¾" x 6¼"
Aida 18	3⅝" x 4⅞"
Hardanger 22	3" x 4"

Stitch Count: 66 x 88

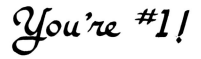

SAMPLE

Stitched on white Linda 27 over two threads, the finished design size is 4½" x 6⅝". (Adjust project measurements for other stitch counts.) Fabric was cut 9" x 11".

MATERIALS FOR ONE BAG

Completed cross-stitch on white Linda 27; matching thread
¼ yard of 45"-wide blue print fabric; matching thread
¾ yard of ⅛"-wide white satin ribbon
Two 5½" x 7" pieces of light-weight cardboard
Dressmakers' pen

DIRECTIONS

All seam allowances are ¼".

1. Cut the Linda 6" x 7½", with the design centered. Cut three 6" x 7½" pieces of blue print fabric.

2. Centering the design, trace the outline of the cardboard on the back of the Linda. Center and trace cardboard on the back of one print fabric piece. Match the right side of the marked Linda with the right side of one un-marked fabric piece. Stitch on the pen line, leaving the entire bottom edge open. Clip the corners and turn right side out. Repeat with the two remaining fabric pieces.

3. Slide a piece of cardboard between the wrong sides of the front and back sections. Tuck lower fabric edges inside and slipstitch.

4. Place the front and back pieces together, with the design facing out. Slipstitch together, leaving the top open to make a pocket.

5. Tie the ribbon in a 3" bow. Tack the bow to the top edge, 1½" from the left corner.

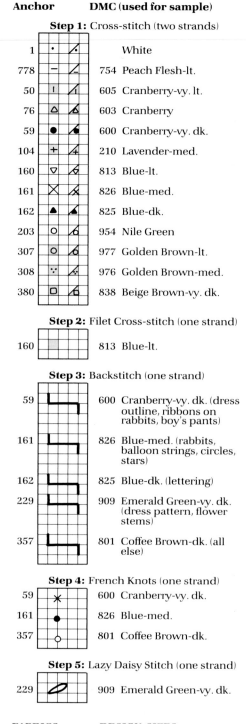

Anchor			DMC (used for sample)

Step 1: Cross-stitch (two strands)

Anchor			DMC	
1	·		White	
778	−		754	Peach Flesh-lt.
50	I		605	Cranberry-vy. lt.
76	△		603	Cranberry
59	●		600	Cranberry-vy. dk.
104	+		210	Lavender-med.
160	▽		813	Blue-lt.
161	✕		826	Blue-med.
162	▲		825	Blue-dk.
203	O		954	Nile Green
307	O		977	Golden Brown-lt.
308	·.·		976	Golden Brown-med.
380	▣		838	Beige Brown-vy. dk.

Step 2: Filet Cross-stitch (one strand)

160		813 Blue-lt.

Step 3: Backstitch (one strand)

59		600 Cranberry-vy. dk. (dress outline, ribbons on rabbits, boy's pants)
161		826 Blue-med. (rabbits, balloon strings, circles, stars)
162		825 Blue-dk. (lettering)
229		909 Emerald Green-vy. dk. (dress pattern, flower stems)
357		801 Coffee Brown-dk. (all else)

Step 4: French Knots (one strand)

59	✳	600 Cranberry-vy. dk.
161	●	826 Blue-med.
357	○	801 Coffee Brown-dk.

Step 5: Lazy Daisy Stitch (one strand)

229	╱	909 Emerald Green-vy. dk.

FABRICS	DESIGN SIZES
Aida 11	5⅝" x 8⅛"
Aida 14	4½" x 6⅜"
Aida 18	3½" x 5"
Hardanger 22	2⅞" x 4⅛"

Stitch Count: 62 x 90

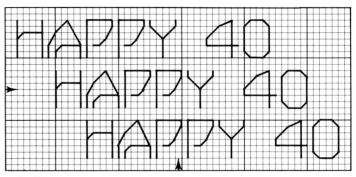

Stitch Count: 34 x 31

A little something for you

SAMPLE

Stitched on a ready-made tote bag using Waste Canvas 14, the finished design size is 2⅜" x 2¼". (Adjust project measurements for other stitch counts.) The waste canvas was cut 4" x 4". See Materials and Directions to make your own bags or refer to Suppliers for information on ordering bags.

MATERIALS FOR TOTE

One 6" x 13" piece of cream canvas; matching thread
½ yard of 1"-wide cream webbing
For Happy 15: 1 yard each of the following ribbons: ¹⁄₁₆"-wide rose, ⅛"-wide lavender, ¼"-wide peach
For Happy 40: 1 yard of ⅛"-wide black polka-dot ribbon

DIRECTIONS

Complete Steps 1–5 of the thank you tote, page 16.

Anchor		DMC (used for sample)
	Step 1:	Backstitch (two strands)
77		602 Cranberry-med. (first row)
98		553 Violet-med. (second row)
941		791 Cornflower Blue-vy. dk. (third row)
		OR
403		310 Black (all rows)

FABRICS	DESIGN SIZES
Aida 11	4⅝" x 2"
Aida 14	3⅝" x 1⅝"
Aida 18	2⅞" x 1¼"
Hardanger 22	2 ⅜" x 1"

Celebrations

SAMPLE

Stitched on white Aida 18, the finished design size is 7⅝″ x 1⅝″. (Adjust project measurements for other stitch counts.) The fabric was cut 14″ x 8″.

MATERIALS FOR SHADOW BOX

Completed cross-stitch
⅜ yard of 45″-wide lavender moiré taffeta
1½ yards of ¼″-wide purple twill tape
One 11″ x 3½″ piece of foamcore board
Memorabilia: a dried flower, a tassel, school pins
One shadow-box frame with a 16″ x 9″ opening (available from a professional framer)
One picture hook or wire
Masking tape
White glue

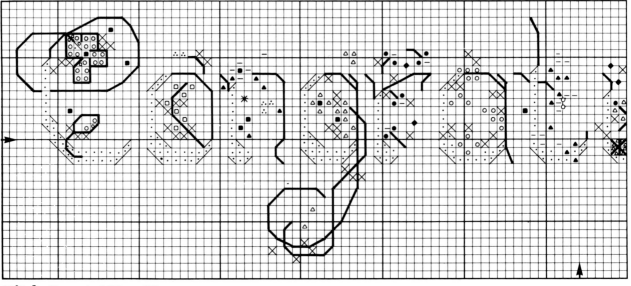

Stitch Count: 138 x 30

DIRECTIONS

1. Place the Aida over the foam-core, with the design centered vertically and the letter *S* positioned 1″ from the right edge. Fold the Aida to the back of the foamcore and glue, keeping the fabric at the corners smooth.

2. Cut one 18″ length from the twill tape. Fold it into two 4″ loops with 7″ or 8″ streamers. Wrap the remaining tape around the left end of the covered foamcore; knot the ends over the center of the loops to make a bow. Pin the knot of the bow 1″ from the top and left edges of the foamcore. Trim twill tape ends.

3. Cut one 19″ x 12″ piece of taffeta lining for the backing piece of the shadow box. Remove backing piece and center the taffeta over it, wrapping the taffeta around the edges. Glue in place.

4. To line the sides, cut a piece of foamcore the same dimensions as each side of the shadow box. Cover with taffeta and glue the covered pieces in place.

5. Arrange the design and memorabilia on the backing piece. Glue, pin, or tack securely. Replace the back of the box and seal it with masking tape. Attach the picture hook or wire.

Anchor **DMC (used for sample)**

Step 1: Cross-stitch (two strands)

Anchor		DMC	
297	⌐	743	Yellow-med.
323	■	722	Orange Spice-lt.
74	o ⟋	3354	Dusty Rose-lt.
42	●	3350	Dusty Rose-vy. dk.
27	∴	899	Rose-med.
95	▫	554	Violet-lt.
101	· ⟋	550	Violet-vy. dk.
130	△	799	Delft-med.
266	▲	471	Avocado Green-vy. lt.
214	✕	368	Pistachio Green-lt.

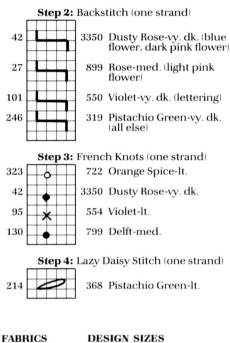

Step 2: Backstitch (one strand)

42		3350	Dusty Rose-vy. dk. (blue flower, dark pink flower)
27		899	Rose-med. (light pink flower)
101		550	Violet-vy. dk. (lettering)
246		319	Pistachio Green-vy. dk. (all else)

Step 3: French Knots (one strand)

323	○	722	Orange Spice-lt.
42	◆	3350	Dusty Rose-vy. dk.
95	✴	554	Violet-lt.
130	●	799	Delft-med.

Step 4: Lazy Daisy Stitch (one strand)

214	⬭	368	Pistachio Green-lt.

FABRICS	DESIGN SIZES
Aida 11	12½″ x 2¾″
Aida 14	9⅞″ x 2⅛″
Hardanger 22	6¼″ x 1⅜″

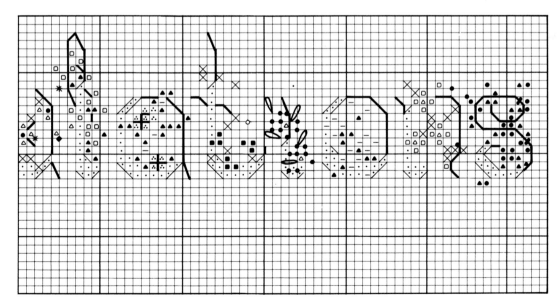

Divorce Greetings

SAMPLE

Stitched on yellow Aida 18, the finished design size is 4⅝″ x 4¼″. (Adjust project measurements for other stitch counts.) The fabric was cut 8″ x 8″.

MATERIALS FOR CARD

Completed cross-stitch
Fusible web
One 7½″ x 12″ piece of black poster board
One small piece of white water-color paper
Lavender colored pencil
White glue
Tracing paper

DIRECTIONS

1. Cut the Aida 6½″ x 5″, with the design centered. Cut a 6½″ x 5″ piece of fusible web.

2. Score the poster board in the center to make a 7½″ x 6″ card. Center and fuse the design piece to the front of the card, according to manufacturer's directions.

3. Trace and cut out the pattern for the heart. Trace the pattern onto the watercolor paper and cut out. Color the heart unevenly with the lavender pencil (see photo). Glue the heart to the upper left corner, ½″ from "drink."

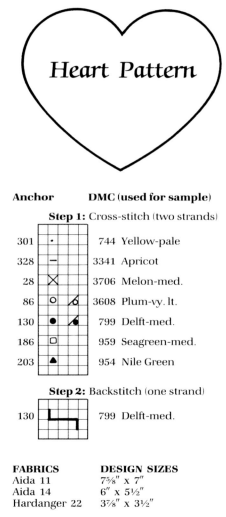

Heart Pattern

Anchor			DMC (used for sample)	
Step 1: Cross-stitch (two strands)				
301	·		744	Yellow-pale
328	−		3341	Apricot
28	✕		3706	Melon-med.
86	○	◸	3608	Plum-vy. lt.
130	●	◢	799	Delft-med.
186	□		959	Seagreen-med.
203	▲		954	Nile Green
Step 2: Backstitch (one strand)				
130			799	Delft-med.

FABRICS	DESIGN SIZES
Aida 11	7⅝″ x 7″
Aida 14	6″ x 5½″
Hardanger 22	3⅞″ x 3½″

Stitch Count: 84 x 77

Applause! Applause!

SAMPLES

Stitched on Natural Linen Plus 28, finished design size of each glove is 3¼" x 1¼". (Adjust project measurements for other stitch counts.) Fabric was cut 6" x 6". A graph is provided for those who prefer to cross-stitch a heart rather than purchase heart beads. (See Suppliers for information on beads.)

MATERIALS FOR ONE PIN

Completed cross-stitch
One small piece of print fabric
One small piece of fusible web
One 1"-wide pin back
One ¾" heart bead (cranberry or frosted pink)
6" of ¹⁄₁₆"-wide satin ribbon to match heart
Water-base varnish

Sponge brush applicator
Glitter spray
Waxed paper
Glue
Large-eyed needle

DIRECTIONS

1. Trim the linen so that it is 1″ larger than the design on all sides. Cut the fusible web and the print fabric the same size as the design piece.

2. Fuse the design piece to the backing, according to the manufacturer's directions.

3. Varnish both sides of the design piece. Pin the edges to waxed paper and allow to dry for at least one hour.

4. Cut carefully, ⅛″ outside of the stitching, following the general shape of the design.

5. Varnish again, covering the raw edges thoroughly. Allow to dry.

6. Spray both the front and the back surfaces with the glitter spray. Allow to dry.

7. To attach the bead, thread the needle with ribbon. Stitch from the back of the design piece to the front, through the bead, and to the back of the design piece again; knot.

8. Glue the pin back to the back of the design piece, securing the ribbon ends.

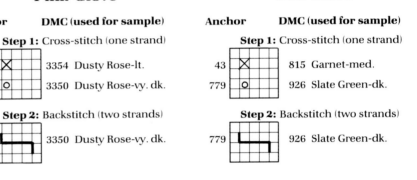

FABRICS   DESIGN SIZES
Aida 11   8⅛″ x 3¼″
Aida 14   6⅜″ x 2⅝″
Aida 18   5″ x 2″
Hardanger 22   4⅛″ x 1⅝″

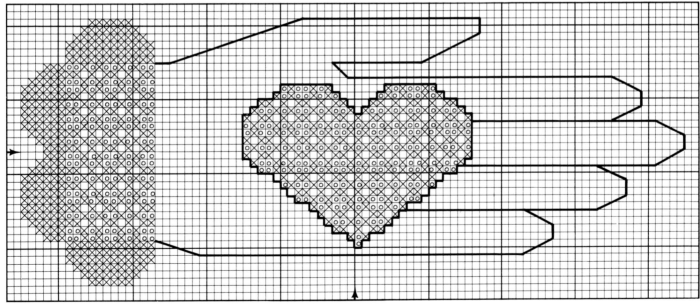

Stitch Count: 90 x 36

here's to you!

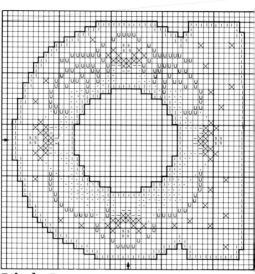

Stitch Count: 45 x 46

Anchor		DMC (used for sample)	
Step 1: Cross-stitch (three strands)			
886	•	677	Old Gold-vy. lt.
892	U	225	Shell Pink-vy. lt.
893	s	224	Shell Pink-lt.
108	I	211	Lavender-lt.
869	−	3042	Antique Violet-lt.
871	▣	3041	Antique Violet-med.
158	O	747	Sky Blue-vy. lt.
159	X	827	Blue-vy. lt.
167	∴	519	Sky Blue
167	N	598	Turquoise-lt.
160	▲	813	Blue-lt.
213	△	504	Blue Green-lt.
213	▢	369	Pistachio Green-vy. lt.
214	+	368	Pistachio Green-lt.
214	Z	966	Baby Green-med.
264	●	472	Avocado Green-ultra lt.
942	B	738	Tan-vy. lt.
397	⧄	453	Shell Gray-lt.
900	E	928	Slate Green-lt.

Step 2: Backstitch (one strand)

101	327	Antique Violet-dk. (violet flowers in 'E', 'K', 'N', 'R')
161	826	Blue-med. (flowers in 'C', design in 'I', 'X')
147	312	Navy Blue-lt. (around letters)

SAMPLE

Stitched on white Perforated Paper 15, the tallest letter is 5⅜" high, and the widest letter is 3¼" across. (Adjust project measurements for other stitch counts.) The paper was cut 5" x 5" for *c, e, r,* and *s,* and 5" x 7" for *h.*

MATERIALS

Completed cross-stitch
1¼ yards of ¹⁄₁₆"-wide blue rayon ribbon
Large-eyed needle

DIRECTIONS

Cut around the outside of each design, one hole away from the backstitching. Thread the ribbon through the needle. Stitch the ribbon through each letter so that letters balance on the ribbon. Tie a loop near the top for hanging.

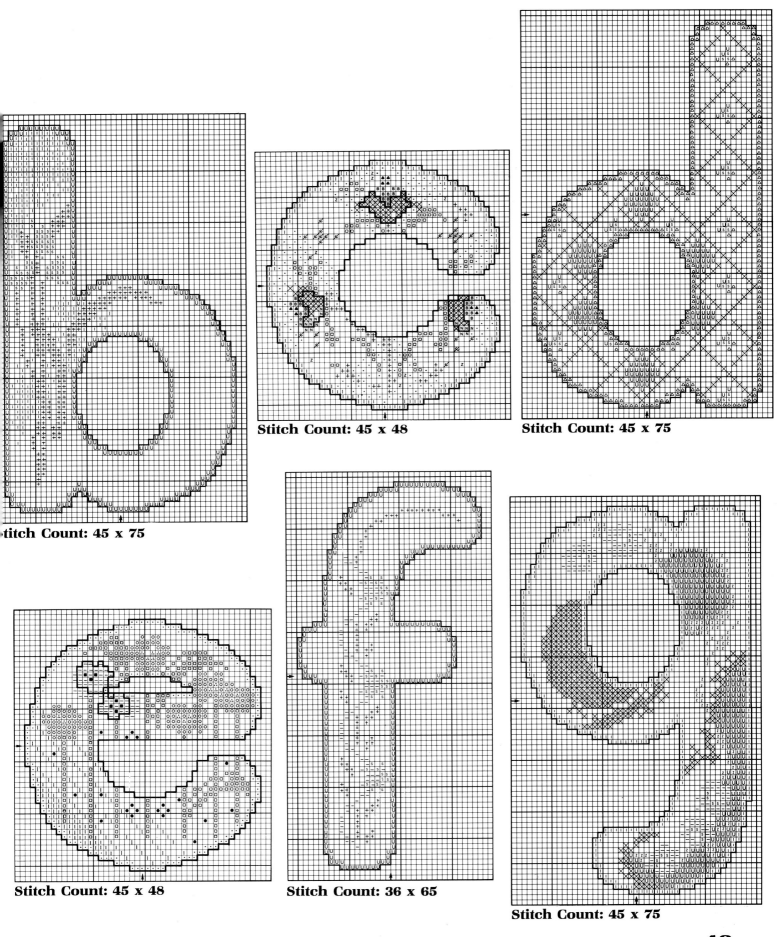

Stitch Count: 45 x 48

Stitch Count: 45 x 75

Stitch Count: 45 x 75

Stitch Count: 45 x 48

Stitch Count: 36 x 65

Stitch Count: 45 x 75

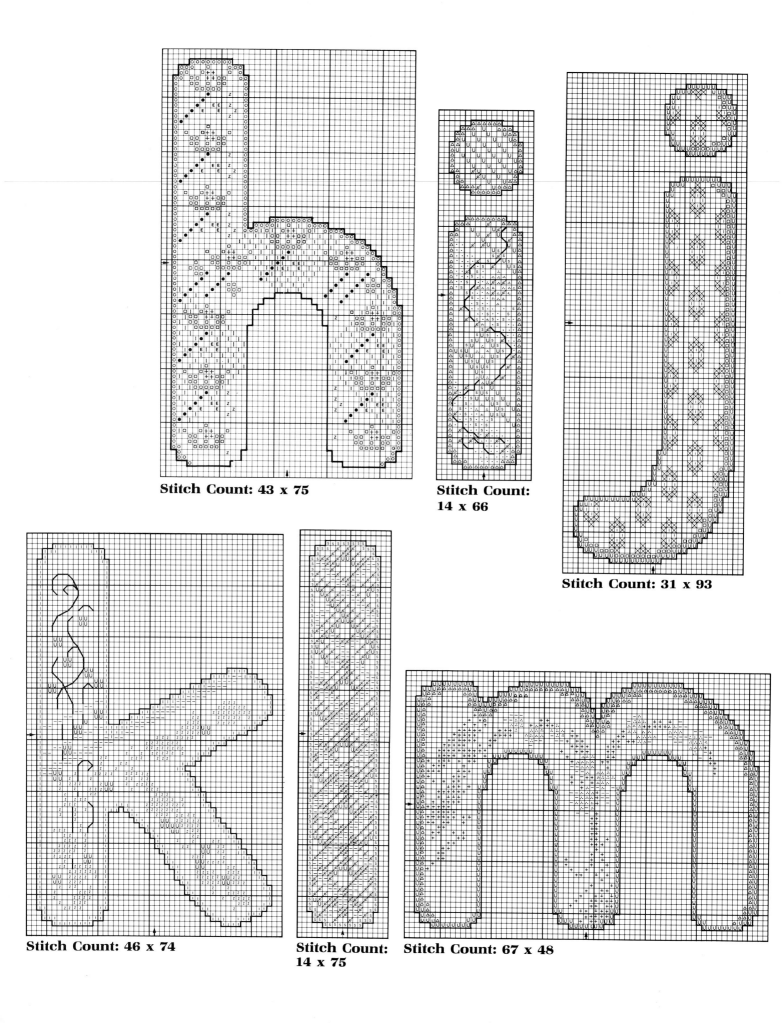

Stitch Count: 43 x 75

**Stitch Count:
14 x 66**

Stitch Count: 31 x 93

Stitch Count: 46 x 74

**Stitch Count:
14 x 75**

Stitch Count: 67 x 48

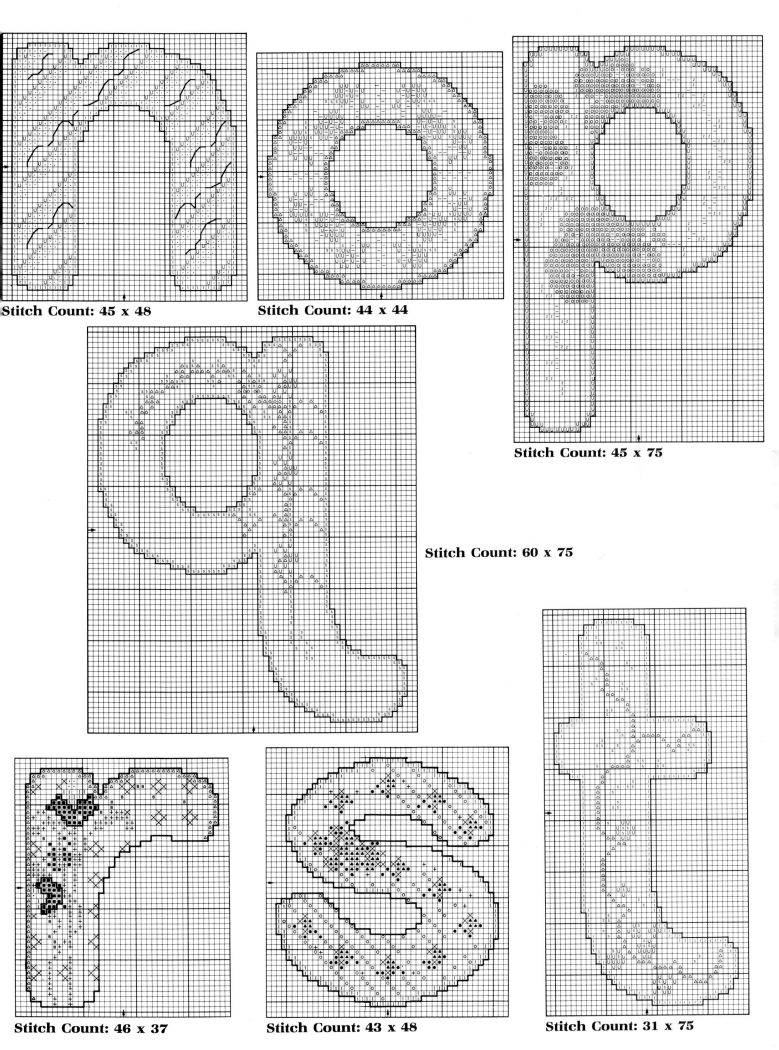

Stitch Count: 45 x 48

Stitch Count: 44 x 44

Stitch Count: 45 x 75

Stitch Count: 60 x 75

Stitch Count: 46 x 37

Stitch Count: 43 x 48

Stitch Count: 31 x 75

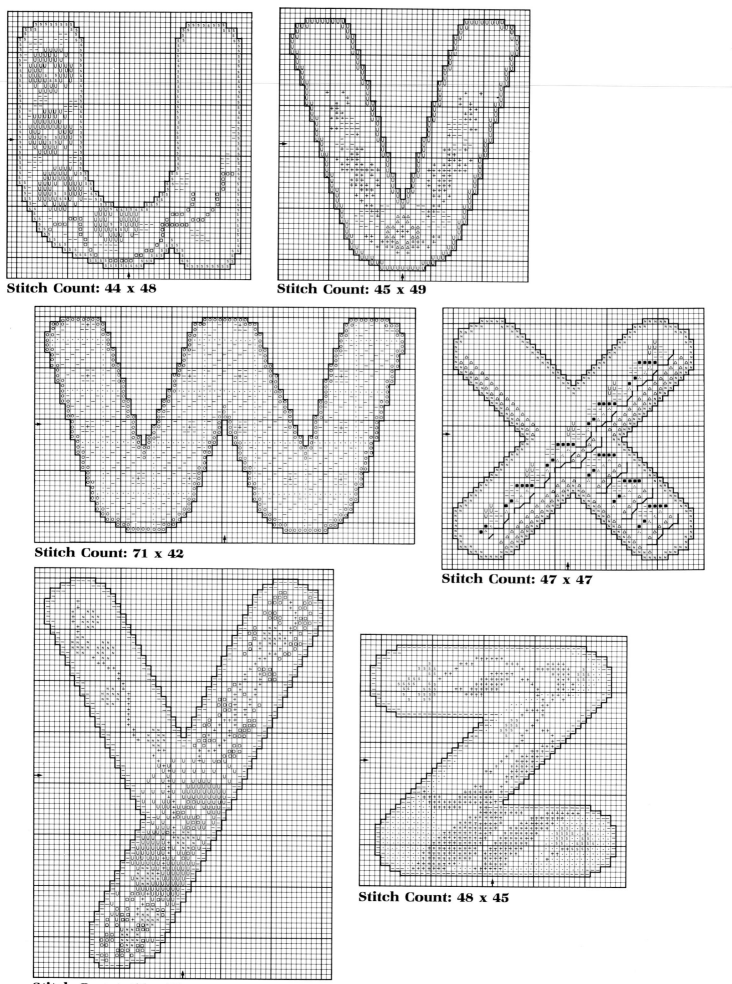

Stitch Count: 44 x 48

Stitch Count: 45 x 49

Stitch Count: 71 x 42

Stitch Count: 47 x 47

Stitch Count: 55 x 76

Stitch Count: 48 x 45

Friendship

A friend is
a neighbor
of the heart

Thanks for popping into my life.

SAMPLE

Stitched on cream Hardanger 22 over two threads, the finished design size is 3¾" x 3⅝". (Adjust project measurements for other stitch counts.) Fabric was cut 8" x 11".

MATERIALS FOR BAG

Completed cross-stitch
One 5½" x 9" piece of unstitched cream Hardanger 22; matching thread
¼ yard of 45"-wide cream/green striped fabric for lining
1 yard of ¼"-wide yellow twill tape
Small amount of polyester fleece
Seam ripper
2 cups of unpopped popcorn

DIRECTIONS

All seam allowances are ¼".

1. Cut the stitched Hardanger 5½" x 9", with the bottom of the design 3" from the bottom edge of the Hardanger. Cut two 5½" x 15" pieces of striped fabric for the lining. Cut two 5½" x 11¾" pieces of polyester fleece.

2. Stitch one lining piece to the top 5½" edge of the stitched Hardanger, right sides together. Repeat with the remaining lining piece and the unstitched Hardanger. Pin the fleece pieces to the wrong sides of the Hardanger pieces, matching the bottom 5½" edges and extending fleece 2½" behind lining (see Diagram).

Anchor		DMC (used for sample)	

Step 1: Cross-stitch (three strands)

295	·	726	Topaz-lt.
307	−	783	Christmas Gold
11	▢	351	Coral
19	O ◪	817	Coral Red-vy. dk.
210	▲	562	Jade-med.
879	✕	890	Pistachio Green-ultra dk.
357	● ◪	801	Coffee Brown-dk.
399	▽ ◪	318	Steel Gray-lt.

Step 2: Backstitch (one strand)

210		562	Jade-med. (lettering)
357		801	Coffee Brown-dk. (tree branches)
403		310	Black (all else)

Step 3: French Knots (one strand)

210	●	562	Jade-med.

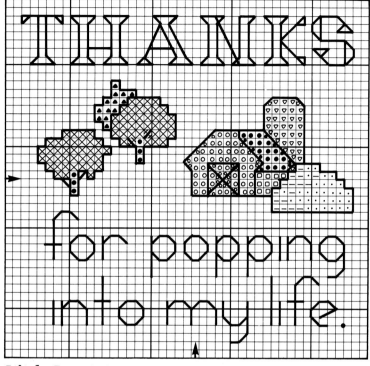

Stitch Count: 41 x 40

FABRICS	DESIGN SIZES
Aida 11	3¾" x 3⅝"
Aida 14	2⅞" x 2⅞"
Aida 18	2¼" x 2¼"
Hardanger 22	1⅞" x 1⅞"

3. Place units right sides together. Stitch entire length of sides and across bottom of Hardanger. Turn bag right side out through opening in end of lining. Slipstitch the opening closed. Fold lining to the inside of the bag and pin with 2¾" of the lining showing above the top of Hardanger.

4. To form the casing, stitch along the seam that joins the lining and the Hardanger. Stitch another seam parallel to and ½" above the first. Using a seam ripper, carefully cut the threads that are between the two rows of stitching on the striped cuff.

5. Cut the twill tape into two equal lengths. Attach a safety pin to the end of one piece and thread it through the opening on one side of the bag, past the second opening, and back out the first opening. Thread the second piece through the second opening, past the first, and out the second. Fill the bag with popcorn. Draw the bag closed and tie the ends of the tape in bows.

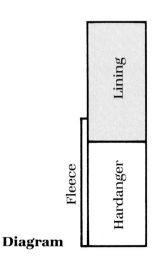

Diagram

You are the apple of my eye.

SAMPLE

Stitched on white Linda 27 over two threads, the finished design size is 3⅝" x 2⅞". (Adjust project measurements for other stitch counts.) The fabric was cut 6" x 8".

MATERIALS FOR BAG

Completed cross-stitch
One 4½" x 6½" piece of un-
    stitched white Linda 27;
    matching thread
⅛ yard of 45"-wide red pindot
    fabric
Small amount of polyester fleece
1¼ yards of ⅛"-wide green
    grosgrain ribbon
Two ½"-wide white wooden
    beads
Seam ripper
Cinnamon sticks

DIRECTIONS

All seam allowances are ¼".

1. Cut the stitched Linda 4½" x 6½", with the bottom of the design 1" from the bottom edge. Cut two 4½" x 9½" pieces of pindot fabric for the lining. Cut two 4½" x 7¾" pieces of fleece.

2. Complete Steps 2 and 3 of the popcorn bag directions, but extend lining 1½" above Linda.

3. Complete Steps 4 and 5 of the directions for the popcorn bag, except use ribbon instead of twill. When the ribbon has been threaded through the casing, thread a bead over the ribbon ends. Knot the ribbon twice and slide the bead to the knot. Repeat for the other side. Fill the bag with the cinnamon sticks.

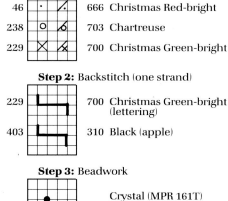

Anchor			DMC (used for sample)

Step 1: Cross-stitch (two strands)

46	·	╱	666 Christmas Red-bright
238	O	◢	703 Chartreuse
229	✕	✖	700 Christmas Green-bright

Step 2: Backstitch (one strand)

| 229 | 700 Christmas Green-bright (lettering) |
| 403 | 310 Black (apple) |

Step 3: Beadwork

| • | Crystal (MPR 161T) |

FABRICS	DESIGN SIZES
Aida 11	4½" x 3⅝"
Aida 14	3½" x 2⅞"
Aida 18	2¾" x 2¼"
Hardanger 22	2¼" x 1⅞"

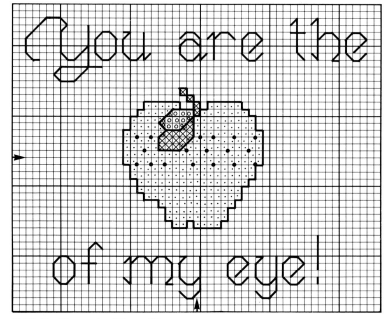

Stitch Count: 49 x 40

a basketful of love

SAMPLE

Stitched on cream Hardanger 22, finished design size is 1⅞" x 1⅞". (Adjust project measurements for other stitch counts.) Fabric was cut 6" x 6". (See Suppliers for information on ordering beads.)

MATERIALS FOR NECKLACE

Completed cross-stitch
One small piece of print fabric
One small piece of fusible web
1 yard of 1/16"-wide pink satin
  ribbon
Four ¾"-wide frosted pink heart
  beads
Two ¾"-wide frosted blue heart
  beads
Nine 6-mm silver rosebud beads
One ⅛"-wide link
Water-base varnish
Sponge brush applicator
Glitter spray
Wax paper

DIRECTIONS

1. Complete Steps 1–6 of the Applause! Applause! pins on page 41.

2. Make a hole in the center top of the design piece, using a pin or needle. Insert the link and close it. Thread the ribbon through the link; match the ends. Thread both ribbon ends through one silver bead. Slide the bead to the top of the link.

3. Tie a knot in each ribbon length, 2½" from the silver bead. Thread beads above knot onto each ribbon in this order: silver, pink, silver, blue, silver, pink, silver (see photo). Knot the ends of the ribbon together.

Anchor		DMC (used for sample)
Step 1: Cross-stitch (one strand)		
893	I	224 Shell Pink-lt.
894	·	223 Shell Pink-med.
897	●	221 Shell Pink-dk.
920	O	932 Antique Blue-lt.
922	X	930 Antique Blue-dk.
Step 2: Backstitch (one strand)		
922		930 Antique Blue-dk.

FABRICS	DESIGN SIZES
Aida 11	3⅝" x 3⅝"
Aida 14	2⅞" x 2⅞"
Aida 18	2¼" x 2¼"

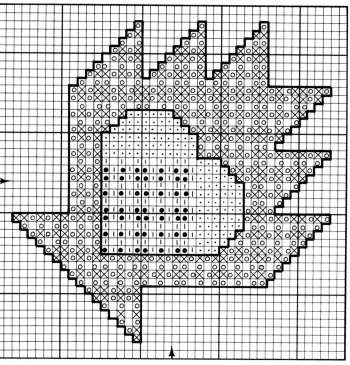

Stitch Count: 40 x 40

ℳ friend is
a neighbor
of the heart.

Ralph Waldo Emerson

SAMPLE

Stitched on cream Hardanger 22 over two threads, the finished design size is 2⅞" x 2". (Adjust project measurements for other stitch counts.) Fabric was cut 16" x 12". Position stitching so center of design is 3½" from left 12" edge and bottom 16" edge.

MATERIALS FOR CARD

Completed cross-stitch
One 8¾" x 12½" piece of tan fabric
1¼ yards of ½"-wide cream rayon seam binding; matching thread
Fusible web
Dressmakers' pen

DIRECTIONS

1. Make a paper pattern and practice the folds before cutting the Hardanger. Mark the fold lines and cutting lines on the Hardanger with the dressmakers' pen. Cut carefully.

2. Cut the Hardanger 8¾" x 12½", with the lower left corner of the design ¼" from the lower left edge and ½" from the bottom edge. Cut the fusible web 8¾" x 12½".

3. Fuse the Hardanger to the lining, according to manufacturer's instructions. Fold the seam binding in half and press. Encase the raw edges of the fabric in the binding. Machine-stitch through all layers, folding the corners of the binding at a 45° angle.

4. Fold the fabric (Diagrams A through D), pressing the folds with a hot iron.

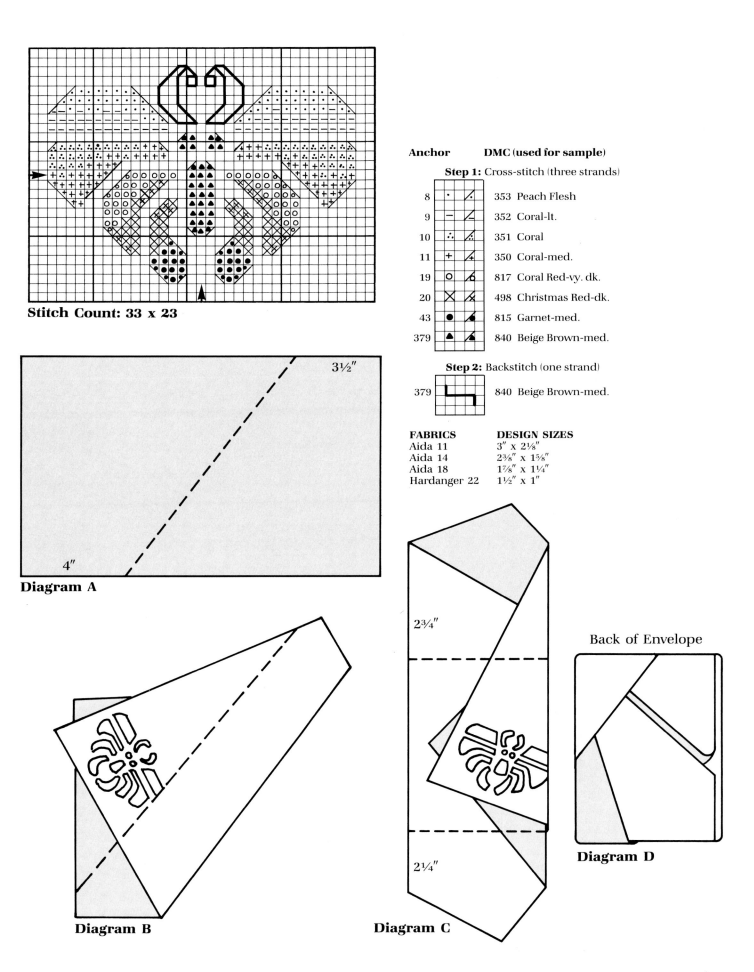

Stitch Count: 33 x 23

Anchor			DMC (used for sample)
		Step 1: Cross-stitch (three strands)	
8	·	⁄	353 Peach Flesh
9	–	⁄	352 Coral-lt.
10	∴	∴⁄	351 Coral
11	+	⁄	350 Coral-med.
19	○	⁄	817 Coral Red-vy. dk.
20	✕	✕	498 Christmas Red-dk.
43	●	⁄	815 Garnet-med.
379	▲	▲	840 Beige Brown-med.

			Step 2: Backstitch (one strand)
379			840 Beige Brown-med.

FABRICS
Aida 11
Aida 14
Aida 18
Hardanger 22

DESIGN SIZES
3″ x 2⅛″
2⅜″ x 1⅝″
1⅞″ x 1¼″
1½″ x 1″

3½″

4″

Diagram A

Diagram B

2¾″

2¼″

Diagram C

Back of Envelope

Diagram D

i go to pieces without you!

SAMPLE

Stitched on gray Glenshee Linen 29 over two threads, finished design size is 6⅛" x 3⅞". (Adjust project measurements for other stitch counts.) Fabric was cut 11" x 9".

MATERIALS FOR CARD

Completed cross-stitch
Small pieces of print fabric; matching thread
8" of ¹⁄₁₆"-wide rose satin ribbon
Three ⅛" navy buttons
One 7" x 5" piece of polyester fleece
Two 7" x 5" pieces of lightweight cardboard
One 7" x 10" piece of gray medium-weight paper
Glue
Transparent tape
Dressmakers' pen
Tracing paper

DIRECTIONS

1. Pin the tracing paper over the stitched design. Make the pattern by outlining the general shape of the cow, ¼" outside the stitching. Cut out.

2. Trace the pattern onto the design piece and cut ¼" outside the pen line. Trace the pattern onto both pieces of cardboard and cut out. Pin the pattern to the polyester fleece and cut out. Fold the 7" x 10" piece of medium-weight paper in half to make a 7" x 5" card. Placing the top of the cow's back on the fold line, trace the pattern

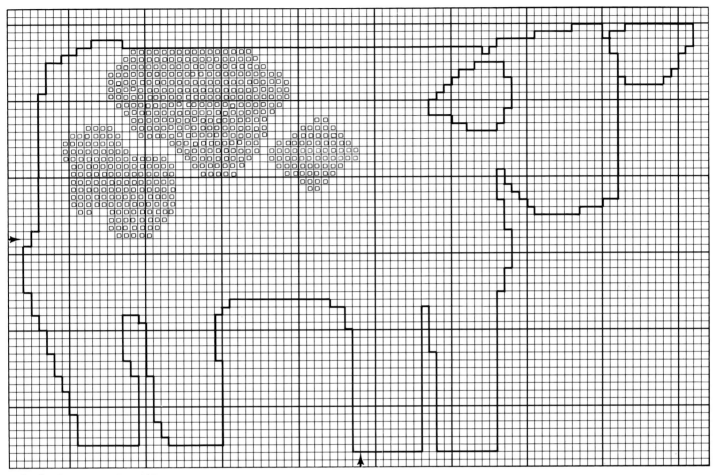

Stitch Count: 88 x 56

onto the paper (the top of the cow's head will extend slightly above the fold line). Cut on the pen lines, but not on the fold.

3. Glue the fleece to the front of one piece of cardboard. Center the design over the fleece and cardboard; pin. Clip the seam allowance to the pen line as needed to wrap the seam allowance to the back of the cardboard. Tape the edges, beginning along the cow's back and continuing all the way around. Glue the remaining piece of cardboard to the back of cow, covering fabric edges.

4. Glue the stuffed cow to the front of the cow-shaped card.

5. Cut five 1¼"-wide circles from print fabric for yo-yos. Turn the edges of two circles ¼" to wrong side; press. Turn the edges of three circles ¼" to the right side; press. Sew a gathering thread around the folded edge of each circle. Gather tightly and secure thread. Press the circles flat with gathered edges in the center. Slipstitch the yo-yos to the cow, gathered edges up (see photo). Glue buttons on. Tie the ribbon into a

bow and slipstitch over the yo-yos. Tack the ribbon ends to the cow.

Anchor		DMC (used for sample)

Step 1: Cross-stitch (two strands)

894 · 223 Shell Pink-med.

Step 2: Backstitch (one strand)

894 · 223 Shell Pink-med.

FABRICS	DESIGN SIZES
Aida 11	8" x 5⅛"
Aida 14	6¼" x 4"
Aida 18	4⅞" x 3⅛"
Hardanger 22	4" x 2½"

SAMPLE

Stitched on gray Glenshee Linen 29 over two threads, the finished design size is 2⅝" x 2⅛". (Adjust project measurements for other stitch counts.) The fabric was cut 6" x 6".

MATERIALS FOR COW

Completed cross-stitch
One 5" x 3½" piece of unstitched gray Belfast Linen 32; matching thread
½ yard of 45"-wide rose fabric; matching thread
⅛ yard of 45"-wide mauve fabric
⅛ yard of 45"-wide pink fabric
1¼ yards of ⅛"-wide rose satin ribbon
Three small bells
Stuffing
Dressmakers' pen
Tracing paper

DIRECTIONS

All seam allowances are ¼″.

1. Trace and cut out the patterns for the cow body, ear, and heart, adding a ¼″ seam allowance.

2. Cut one cow body, four ear pieces, and twenty 2″ x 2″ blocks from the rose fabric. Cut thirty-one 2″ x 2″ blocks from the mauve fabric and twelve 2″ x 2″ blocks from the pink fabric.

3. Stitch the blocks together (see Diagram). Cut one cow body from the pieced blocks.

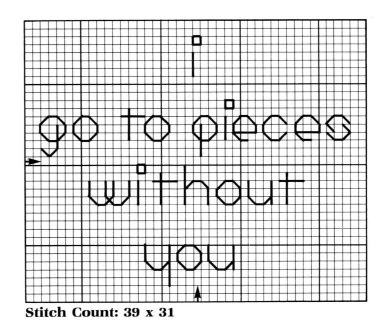

☐ — Rose
☒ — Mauve
☐ — Pink

4. Pin two ear pieces, right sides together and raw edges aligned. Stitch, leaving an opening for turning. Clip curves. Turn right side out and slipstitch the opening closed. Repeat for the second pair of ear pieces.

5. Pin the two body pieces, right sides together and raw edges aligned. Stitch, leaving an opening for turning. Clip curves. Turn right side out and stuff firmly. Slipstitch the opening closed. To make the front legs, stitch through both layers along the stitching line on the right side of the cow. Backstitch to secure.

6. Tack the ears securely to the cow (see photo).

7. Center the heart pattern over the stitched design on the linen and cut it out for the front. Cut one piece for the back from the unstitched linen.

8. Pin the two heart pieces, right sides together and raw edges aligned. Stitch, leaving an opening for turning. Clip curves. Turn right side out and stuff firmly. Slipstitch the opening closed.

9. Cut one 8″ length and one 14″ length of ribbon. Make a 6″ loop in the center of the remaining ribbon and across the ends. Tie the 14″ length around the cow's neck and knot. Tie the ends around the center of the 6″ loop to make a bow. Fold the 8″ length in half and knot the ends. Tack the knot to the center back of the heart. Slide three bells over the ribbon. Knot again above the bells. Tie this ribbon to the ribbon around the cow's neck.

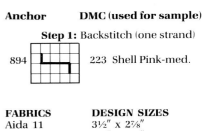

Anchor		DMC (used for sample)
	Step 1: Backstitch (one strand)	
894		223 Shell Pink-med.

FABRICS	DESIGN SIZES
Aida 11	3½″ x 2⅞″
Aida 14	2¾″ x 2¼″
Aida 18	2⅛″ x 1¾″
Hardanger 22	1¾″ x 1⅜″

Stitch Count: 39 x 31

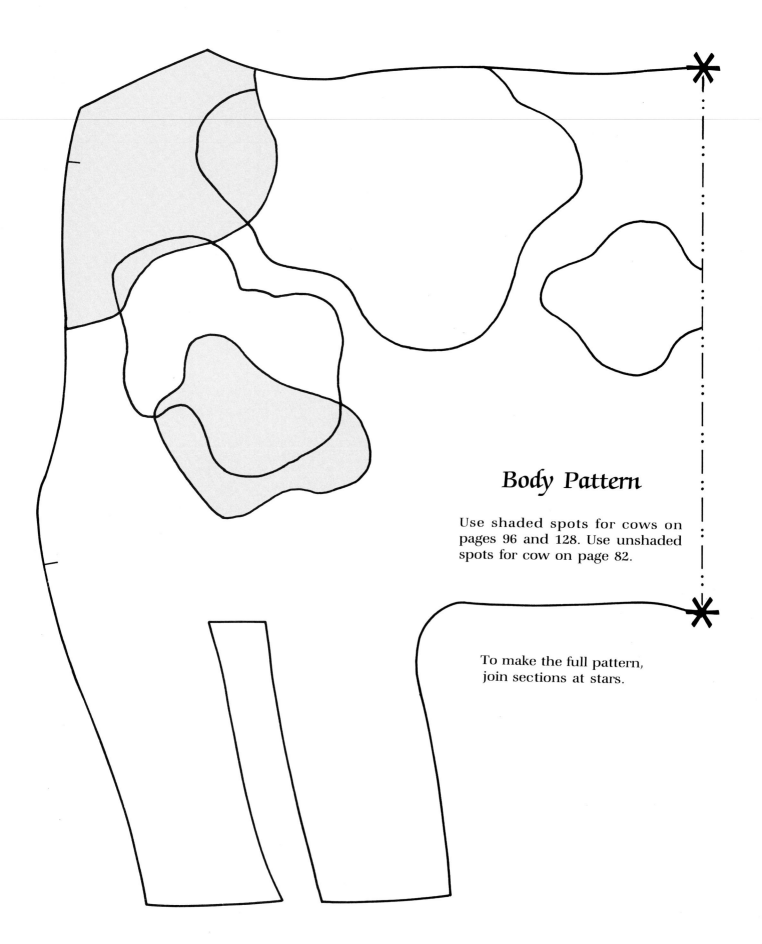

Body Pattern

Use shaded spots for cows on pages 96 and 128. Use unshaded spots for cow on page 82.

To make the full pattern, join sections at stars.

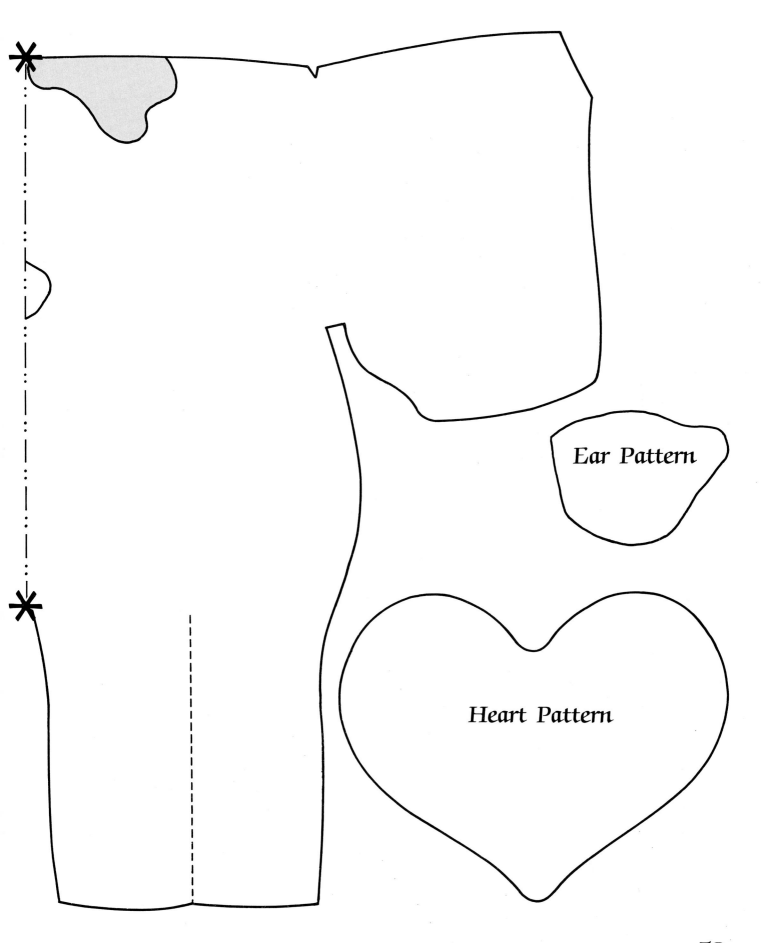

Ear Pattern

Heart Pattern

Let me give you a hand.

SAMPLE

Stitched on cream Belfast Linen 32 over two threads, the finished design size is 3″ x 1⅜″. (Adjust project measurements for other stitch counts.) Fabric was cut 10″ x 10″.

MATERIALS FOR HANGER

Completed cross-stitch
One 8″ square piece of un-stitched cream Belfast Linen; matching thread
½ yard of ¼″-wide cream satin ribbon
1 yard of double-fold cream satin bias tape
One 6¾″-wide wire clothes hanger
Dressmakers' pen
Tracing paper
Purchased or hand-knit gloves

DIRECTIONS

1. Trace the outline of the hanger onto paper. Place the pattern over the stitched linen, centering the design horizontally and 3″ above the lower edge of the fabric. Add a ¼″ seam allowance at all edges, except ½″ at the neck; cut. Also cut a matching piece for the back from the unstitched linen.

2. On the lower edge of the front, fold ¼″ to the wrong side; then fold again. Machine-stitch close to the folded edge. Repeat on the back piece.

3. Fold ½″ to the wrong side at the neck, on both the front and the back pieces. Press. Pin the front to the back piece, right sides together and raw edges aligned. Stitch, leaving the neck and the hemmed edges open. Clip curves. Turn right side out and press.

4. Wrap the satin bias tape around the bottom of the hanger and ½″ up each side. Secure the ends with glue or tack securely. Also wrap and secure the bias tape around the hook and neck of the hanger.

5. Slide the design piece over the neck, keeping seam allowances turned under. Slipstitch the two hemmed edges together.

6. Cut a 5″ length of ribbon. Fold a 4″ loop in the remaining ribbon. Tie the 5″ length around the hanger neck and then around the center of the ribbon loop to make a bow. Trim the ends. Attach gloves to the ribbons and drape them over the hanger.

Anchor	DMC (used for sample)
Step 1: Backstitch (one strand)	
894	223 Shell Pink-med.
Step 2: French Knots (one strand)	
894	223 Shell Pink-med.

FABRICS	DESIGN SIZES
Aida 11	4¼″ x 1⅞″
Aida 14	3⅜″ x 1½″
Aida 18	2⅝″ x 1⅛″
Hardanger 22	2⅛″ x 1″

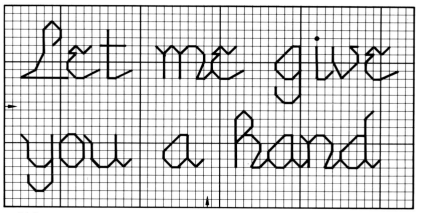

Stitch Count: 47 x 21

Just Because

Aida horizontally on the green fabric, with the design ⅝″ above the bottom edge of the card. Fuse the Aida to the green fabric.

3. Trace and cut out the patterns for the rainbow and the heart. Transfer each design three times to the small pieces of poster board; then color and cut out. Glue the rainbows to the front of the card and the hearts on the rainbows (see photo).

4. Cut each piece of ribbon into two equal lengths. Handling all the ribbon pieces as one, tie a wide bow. Glue the bow to the upper left corner of the front of the card. Trim the ends to irregular lengths.

Keep Smiling!

Patterns

SAMPLE

Stitched on light blue Aida 14, the finished design size is 5″ x 6⅜″. (Adjust project measurements for other stitch counts.) The fabric was cut 9″ x 10″.

MATERIALS FOR CARD

Completed cross-stitch
One 6⅞″ x 8⅞″ piece of green fabric
One 13¾″ x 8⅞″ piece of white poster board
Small pieces of white poster board
2½ yards each of the following ribbons: ⅛″-wide lavender satin, ¹⁄₁₆″-wide white satin, ¹⁄₁₆″-wide pink rayon braid, ¹⁄₁₆″-wide yellow rayon braid

Fusible web
Colored pencils: yellow, red, blue, green, orange, lavender
Rubber cement
Tracing paper
One small piece of graphite paper

DIRECTIONS

1. Cut the Aida 6⅜″ x 8″, with the design centered. Cut one piece of fusible web 6⅞″ x 8⅞″ and one piece 6⅜″ x 8″.

2. Score the large piece of poster board to make a 6⅞″ x 8⅞″ card. Using the larger piece of fusible web and following manufacturer's directions, fuse the green fabric to the front of the card. Center the

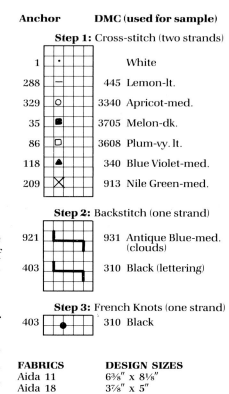

Anchor		DMC (used for sample)
		Step 1: Cross-stitch (two strands)
1	·	White
288	–	445 Lemon-lt.
329	o	3340 Apricot-med.
35	■	3705 Melon-dk.
86	▫	3608 Plum-vy. lt.
118	▲	340 Blue Violet-med.
209	✕	913 Nile Green-med.
		Step 2: Backstitch (one strand)
921		931 Antique Blue-med. (clouds)
403		310 Black (lettering)
		Step 3: French Knots (one strand)
403	●	310 Black

FABRICS	DESIGN SIZES
Aida 11	6⅜″ x 8⅛″
Aida 18	3⅞″ x 5″
Hardanger 22	3⅛″ x 4⅛″

FINDING A RAINBOW
IN A CLOUD
IS EASY....
KEEPING IT
IS HARD TO DO

Stitch Count: 70 x 90

*Life is like a rosebud
waiting to unfold,
Each petal holds a secret
waiting to be told.
Author Unknown*

MATERIALS FOR ENVELOPE

Completed cross-stitch
One 8¾" x 12½" piece of print fabric
1¼ yards of tan rayon seam binding; matching thread
Fusible web
Dressmakers' pen

DIRECTIONS

1. Complete steps 1–4 of the butterfly envelope, shown on page 52.

Stitch Count: 44 x 40

Anchor		DMC (used for sample)
Step 1: Cross-stitch (two strands)		
49	−	3689 Mauve-lt.
66	o	3688 Mauve-med.
69	●	3687 Mauve
213	·	369 Pistachio Green-vy. lt.
214	X	368 Pistachio Green-lt.
215	■	320 Pistachio Green-med.

Anchor		DMC (used for sample)
Step 2: Backstitch (one strand)		
69		3687 Mauve (rose)
216		367 Pistachio Green-dk. (leaves)

FABRICS	DESIGN SIZES
Aida 11	4" x 3⅝"
Aida 14	3⅛" x 2⅞"
Aida 18	2½" x 2¼"
Hardanger 22	2" x 1⅞"

Violets bloom
where
they find room.

SAMPLE

Stitched on Glenshee Egyptian Cotton quality D over two threads, the finished design size is 6½" x 4⅛". (Adjust project measurements for other stitch counts.) The fabric was cut 11" x 9".

MATERIALS FOR CARD

Completed cross-stitch
One 10½" x 17½" piece of cream watercolor paper
One 10½" x 8¾" piece of cream watercolor paper
One 12" x 10" piece of light-weight tan fabric; matching thread
Fusible web
Rubber cement
Dressmakers' pen
Tracing paper

DIRECTIONS

1. Trace and cut out the pattern for window. Center pattern on the tan fabric and trace with the dressmakers' pen. Cut ¼" inside the scalloped edge. Clip curves.

2. Center the fabric over the stitched design. Fold under the seam allowance and pin. Slip-stitch the scalloped edges to the Glenshee. Sew a small running stitch ⅛" inside the scalloped edge. Remove all pen marks.

3. Cut the fabric and the Glenshee 10" x 8¼", with the design centered. Cut one 10" x 8¼" piece of fusible web.

4. For the mat, mark a 9" x 7¼" window in the center of the back of the 10½" x 8¾" piece of paper and cut out.

5. Score the 10½" x 17½" piece of paper in the center to make a 10½" x 8¾" card. Center and fuse the design to the card front, according to manufacturer's instructions. Rubber-cement the mat over the fabric, sealing the edges of the mat to the card front.

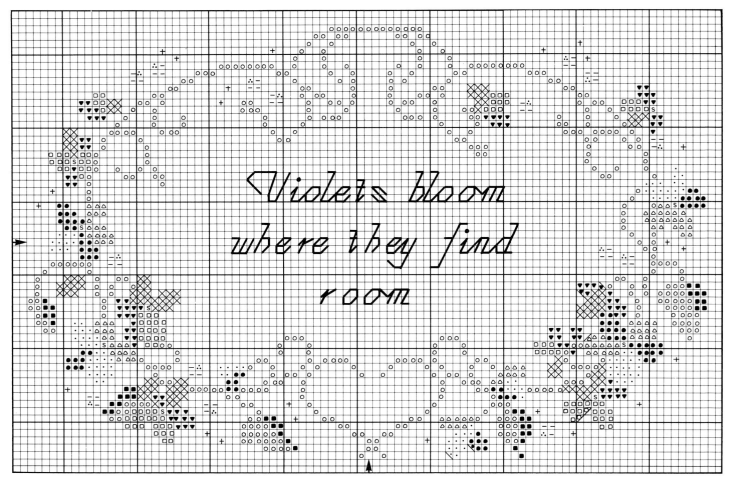

Stitch Count: 93 x 59

Window Pattern

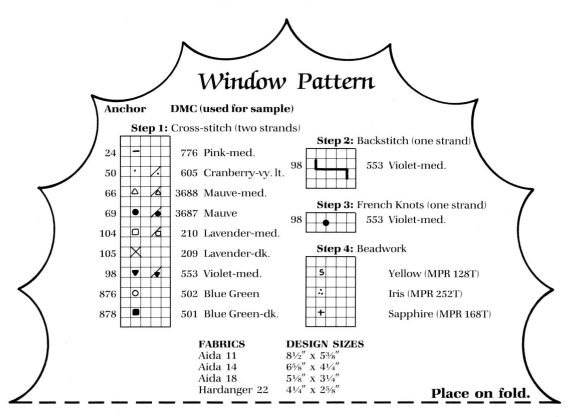

Anchor		DMC (used for sample)

Step 1: Cross-stitch (two strands)

24	−		776	Pink-med.
50	·	╱	605	Cranberry-vy. lt.
66	△	◣	3688	Mauve-med.
69	●	◕	3687	Mauve
104	□	◸	210	Lavender-med.
105	✕		209	Lavender-dk.
98	▼	◢	553	Violet-med.
876	○		502	Blue Green
878	■		501	Blue Green-dk.

Step 2: Backstitch (one strand)

98   553 Violet-med.

Step 3: French Knots (one strand)

98   553 Violet-med.

Step 4: Beadwork

s	Yellow (MPR 128T)
∴	Iris (MPR 252T)
+	Sapphire (MPR 168T)

FABRICS	DESIGN SIZES
Aida 11	8½″ x 5⅜″
Aida 14	6⅝″ x 4¼″
Aida 18	5⅛″ x 3¼″
Hardanger 22	4¼″ x 2⅝″

Place on fold.

To create a little flower is the labor of the ages.

William Blake

SAMPLE

Stitched on white Belfast Linen 32 over two threads, the finished design size is 4½" x 4⅝". (Adjust project measurements for other stitch counts.) Fabric was cut 8" x 10".

Anchor		DMC (used for sample)	
Step 1: Cross-stitch (two strands)			
8	·	353	Peach Flesh
10	△	352	Coral-lt.
11	■	350	Coral-med.
24	I	776	Pink-med.
25	□	3326	Rose-lt.
42	●	335	Rose
117	∩	341	Blue Violet-lt.
118	+	340	Blue Violet-med.
213	·	369	Pistachio Green-vy. lt.
214	−	368	Pistachio Green-lt.
215	✕	320	Pistachio Green-med.
264	○	472	Avocado Green-ultra lt.
266	∴	471	Avocado Green-vy. lt.
267	▲	470	Avocado Green-lt.
378	✕	841	Beige Brown-lt.

Anchor		DMC (used for sample)	
Step 2: Backstitch (one strand)			
879	⌐	500	Blue Green-vy. dk. (narrow stems)
905	⌐	645	Beaver Gray-vy. dk. (all else)

FABRICS	DESIGN SIZES
Aida 11	6⅜" x 6¾"
Aida 14	5" x 5¼"
Aida 18	3⅞" x 4⅛"
Hardanger 22	3⅛" x 3⅜"

MATERIALS FOR CARD

Completed cross-stitch
¼"-wide variegated ribbon and matching thread: 4" of yellow, 4" of blue, 6" of lavender, 8" of pink
Fusible web
One 13" x 8" piece of poster board
6½" x 8" piece of watercolor paper
Rust or brown watercolor paint
Green colored pencil
Paintbrush
Rubber cement

Stitch Count: 70 x 74

DIRECTIONS

1. Cut the linen 5¾" x 7¼", with the design centered. Cut a piece of fusible web 5¾" x 7¼".

2. Score the poster board in the center to make a 6½" x 8" card. Center and fuse the linen to the front of the card, according to manufacturer's directions.

3. Paint the watercolor paper with a light wash of the watercolor paint.

4. Mark a 4½" x 6" window on the back of the watercolor paper. Cut out the window to make a mat. Using the green pencil, lightly draw a line around the mat, ¼" from and parallel to the window. Glue the mat to the front of the card.

5. Cut the ribbon into 2" lengths. To make a ribbon flower, sew a small running stitch close to one edge of a piece of ribbon. Gather

tightly, tucking the raw ends under and securing the thread (see Diagram). Repeat for each 2" piece of ribbon. Glue the flowers to the front of the card (see photo).

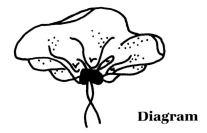

Diagram

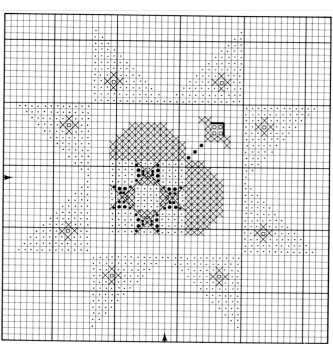

Stitch Count: 48 x 48

Starlight, Starbright... Hope, love and dreams are yours tonight.

SAMPLE

Stitched on cream Hardanger 22, the finished design size is 2⅛" x 2⅛". (Adjust project measurements for other stitch counts.) The fabric was cut 6" x 6".

MATERIALS FOR NECKLACE

Completed cross-stitch
One small piece of print fabric
One small piece of fusible web
1 yard of ¹⁄₁₆"-wide cranberry
   satin ribbon
One 6-mm silver rosebud bead
One ⅛"-wide link
Water-base varnish

Sponge brush applicator
Glitter spray
Wax paper

DIRECTIONS

1. Complete Steps 1–6 of the Applause! Applause! pins on page 41.

2. Make a hole in the center top of the design piece, using a pin or needle. Insert the link and close it. Thread the ribbon through the link; match the ends. Thread both ribbon ends through the bead. Slide the bead to the top of the link. Knot the ends of the ribbon together.

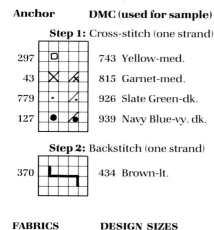

Anchor		DMC (used for sample)
	Step 1: Cross-stitch (one strand)	
297	▢	743 Yellow-med.
43	✕	815 Garnet-med.
779	·	926 Slate Green-dk.
127	●	939 Navy Blue-vy. dk.
	Step 2: Backstitch (one strand)	
370	⌐	434 Brown-lt.

FABRICS	DESIGN SIZES
Aida 11	4⅜" x 4⅜"
Aida 14	3⅜" x 3⅜"
Aida 18	2⅝" x 2⅝"

Love

Please Write!  Heart Pattern

SAMPLE

Stitched on white Linda 27 over two threads, the finished design size is 9⅜" x 5½". (Adjust project measurements for other stitch counts.) Fabric was cut 12" x 23".

MATERIALS FOR PILLOW

Completed cross-stitch; matching thread
One small piece of pink print fabric; matching thread
10" of ⅛"-wide white rickrack; matching thread
½ yard of ½"-wide white heart-design lace
Stuffing
Dressmakers' pen
Tracing paper

DIRECTIONS

All seam allowances are ¼".

1. Cut Linda 10½" x 21", with design centered vertically. At the top edge, cut the point for the flap (see Diagram). Zigzag along the bottom 10½" edge. Cut rickrack into four equal lengths. Position the lengths in four evenly spaced rows (see photo). Tack in place.

2. Fold up the lower 7" of fabric over the design, right sides together. Stitch both side edges. Turn right side out and stuff. Slipstitch the opening closed.

3. Fold under ½" along the envelope flap. Slipstitch the flap to the back of the pillow.

Diagram

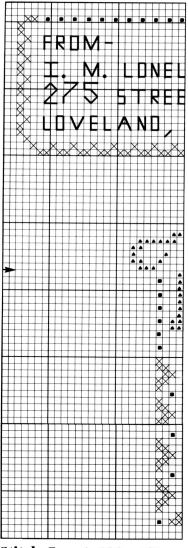

Stitch Count: 126 x 76

4. Trace and cut out the pattern for the heart. Cut the heart from the pink print fabric, adding a ¼" seam allowance. Fold the seam allowance under. Place the tip of the heart ¾" above the point on the flap; appliqué in place.

5. Slipstitch the lace along the edges of the flap.

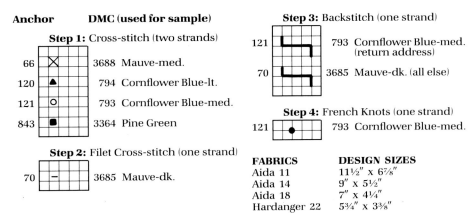

Anchor		DMC (used for sample)

Step 1: Cross-stitch (two strands)

66	☒	3688 Mauve-med.
120	▲	794 Cornflower Blue-lt.
121	○	793 Cornflower Blue-med.
843	■	3364 Pine Green

Step 2: Filet Cross-stitch (one strand)

| 70 | − | 3685 Mauve-dk. |

Step 3: Backstitch (one strand)

| 121 | | 793 Cornflower Blue-med. (return address) |
| 70 | | 3685 Mauve-dk. (all else) |

Step 4: French Knots (one strand)

| 121 | ● | 793 Cornflower Blue-med. |

FABRICS	DESIGN SIZES
Aida 11	11½" x 6⅞"
Aida 14	9" x 5½"
Aida 18	7" x 4¼"
Hardanger 22	5¾" x 3⅜"

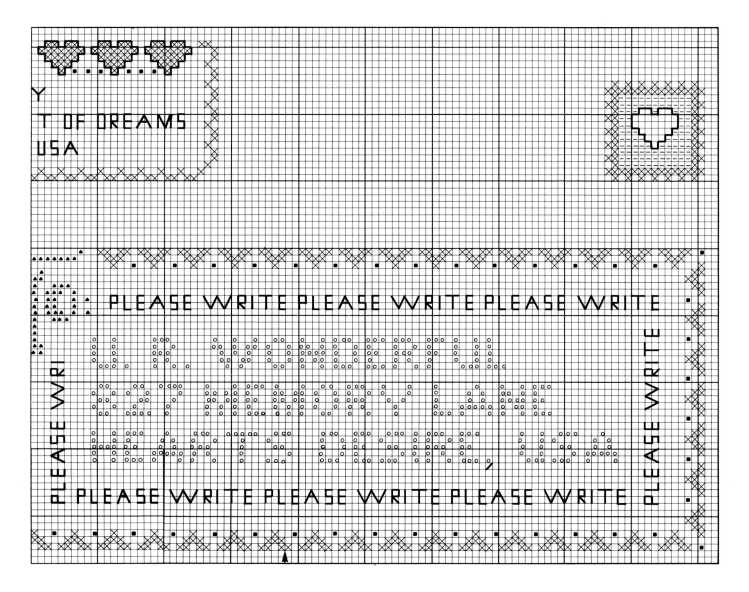

i miss you!

SAMPLES

CARD: Stitched on white Aida 18, the finished design size is 4⅞" x 3½". (Adjust project measurements for other stitch counts.) The fabric was cut 10" x 9".

T-SHIRT: The design is stitched on a purchased white knit shirt, using Waste Canvas 14. The finished design size is 2" x 1⅞". The waste canvas was cut 5" x 5". Using the graph for the greeting card, stitch the left teddy bear only, positioning the stitching as desired on the front of the shirt (see photo).

MATERIALS FOR CARD

Completed cross-stitch
½ yard of 45"-wide blue-gray print fabric; matching thread
Fusible web
One 8" x 14" piece of white poster board
One 7½" x 13½" piece of white paper
Rubber cement
Dressmakers' pen
Tracing paper

DIRECTIONS

1. Cut the Aida 8" x 7", with the design centered.

2. Cut one 10" x 15" piece from the print fabric. Also cut a 1½"-wide bias strip, piecing as needed to equal 20".

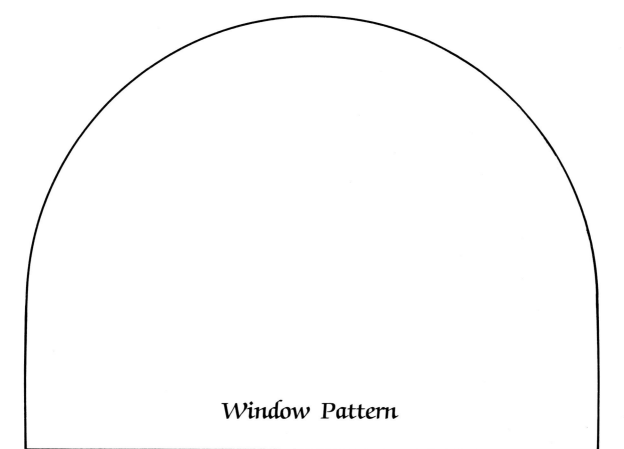

Window Pattern

3. Cut one 8″ x 13″ piece of fusible web.

4. Score the piece of white poster board in the center to make an 8″ x 7″ card.

5. Stitch gathering threads along one long edge of the bias strip. Gather to make a 9″ ruffle. Place the ruffle across the front of the card, keeping the ungathered raw edge even with the bottom edge of the card. Wrap the ends of the ruffle around the side edges of the card. Sew or glue the gathered edge to the card.

6. Trace and cut out the pattern for the window. Trace the pattern onto the 10″ x 15″ piece of print fabric, with the straight edge of the window 2″ from one 10″ edge of the fabric.

7. Cut ¼″ inside the pen line of the window. Clip the curved edge. Center the window over the design. Fold the seam allowance under and slipstitch the fabric to the design piece. Trim the design piece on the wrong side so that it is ¼″ larger than the window.

8. Fold ¾″ of the print fabric to the wrong side along the bottom

10″ edge. Center the fusible web behind the fabric, inserting one 8″ edge of the fusible web into the fold. Fuse the print fabric to the card, according to manufacturer's instructions. (The fold covers the gathered edge of the ruffle.) Fold excess fabric on sides and back to the inside of the card and secure all edges with rubber cement.

9. Fold the white paper in the center to measure 7½″ x 6¾″. Place paper inside the card, matching the fold line to the score line. Secure with rubber cement along the score line and the corners, hiding the raw edges of the fabric.

Stitch Count: 88 x 64

Anchor		DMC (used for sample)

Step 1: Cross-stitch (two strands)

1	· /	White
292	▽ /	3078 Golden Yellow-vy. lt.
307	✕ /	977 Golden Brown-lt.
24	· /	776 Pink-med.
76	● /	603 Cranberry
158	– /	775 Baby Blue-lt.
941	○ /	791 Cornflower Blue-vy. dk.

213	I /	504 Blue Green-lt.
373	+ /	422 Hazel Nut Brown-lt.
379	/	840 Beige Brown-med.
380	✕ /	839 Beige Brown-dk.

Step 2: Backstitch (one strand)

| 941 | ⌐ | 791 Cornflower Blue-vy. dk. (lettering) |
| 381 | ⌐ | 938 Coffee Brown-ultra dk. (all else) |

Step 3: French Knots (one strand)

| 381 | ● | 938 Coffee Brown-ultra dk. |

FABRICS — **DESIGN SIZES**
Aida 11 — 8" x 5¾"
Aida 14 — 6¼" x 4⅝"
Hardanger 22 — 4" x 2⅞"

You're the Best!

SAMPLE

Stitched on white Belfast Linen 32 over two threads, the finished design size is 3¾" x 4⅜". (Adjust project measurements for other stitch counts.) The fabric was cut 8" x 8".

MATERIALS FOR CARD

Completed cross-stitch
Fusible web
One 6½" x 14" piece of medium-weight glossy white paper
One 5¾" x 6½" piece of watercolor paper
Watercolor paint: red, green, pink
Small and medium-size paint-brushes
Purple colored pencil
White glue
Tracing paper
One small piece of graphite paper

DIRECTIONS

1. Cut the linen 5¼" x 5½", with the design centered. Cut one piece of fusible web 5¼" x 5½".

2. Score the white paper in the center to make a 6½" x 7" card.

3. Center and fuse the linen to the front of the card, according to manufacturer's directions.

4. Using the medium-size brush, paint the watercolor paper for the mat with a thin wash of red paint.

5. Mark a 4" x 4⅝" window on the back of the watercolor paper. Cut out the window to make the mat.

6. Trace and cut out the pattern for the flower design on page 78. Transfer the design to the front of the mat, using the graphite paper and light pencil lines. Using the small brush, paint the flowers in varying shades of red and pink so that they are somewhat darker

than the background. Paint the stems and leaves with the green paint.

7. Outline each flower with the purple colored pencil. Also draw a line around the mat, ⅛" from and parallel to the window. Still using the purple pencil, color the space between the line and the window edge to make a border. Center and glue the mat to the card front.

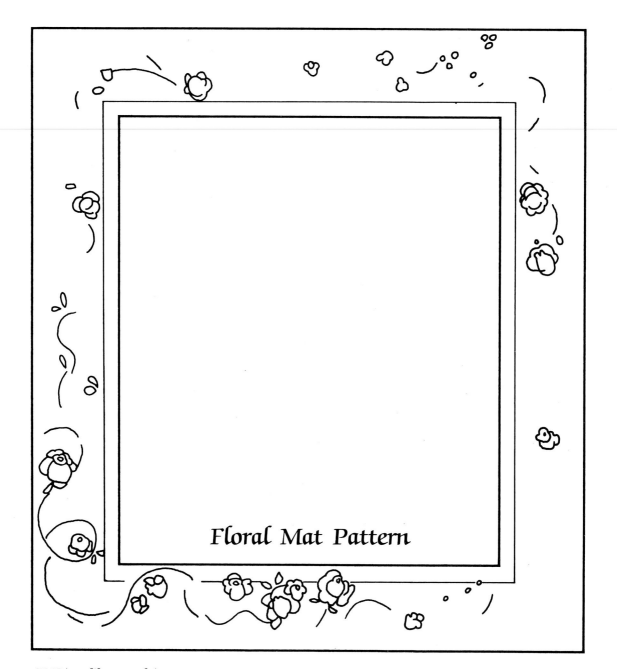

Floral Mat Pattern

Anchor   **DMC (used for sample)**

Step 1: Cross-stitch (two strands)

Anchor			DMC
1	·	∕·	White
386	H	∕H	746 Off White
301	Z	∕Z	744 Yellow-pale
328	△	◿	3341 Apricot
329	E	∕E	3340 Apricot-med.
25	∴	∕∴	3326 Rose-lt.
27	N	∕N	899 Rose-med.
42	S	∕S	335 Rose
43	✕		3350 Dusty Rose-vy. dk.
70	▲		3685 Mauve-dk.

Anchor			DMC
108	Γ	⊼	211 Lavender-lt.
95	K	⊼	554 Violet-lt.
110	■	◢	208 Lavender-vy. dk.
158	U	⊿	747 Sky Blue-vy. lt.
130	B		799 Delft-med.
131	∕⁄		798 Delft-dk.
187	O	◿	992 Aquamarine
189	●	◢	991 Aquamarine-dk.
208	∤		563 Jade-lt.
210	▢		562 Jade-med.
212	+		561 Jade-vy. dk.

Step 2: Backstitch (one strand)

Anchor		DMC
304		741 Tangerine-med. (yellow flowers)
70		3685 Mauve-dk. (lettering)
130		799 Delft-med. (blue flowers)
189		991 Aquamarine-dk. (stems)

Step 3: French Knots (one strand)

Anchor		DMC
70	●	3685 Mauve-dk.

FABRICS	DESIGN SIZES
Aida 11	5½" x 6⅜"
Aida 14	4¼" x 5"
Aida 18	3⅜" x 3⅞"
Hardanger 22	2¾" x 3⅛"

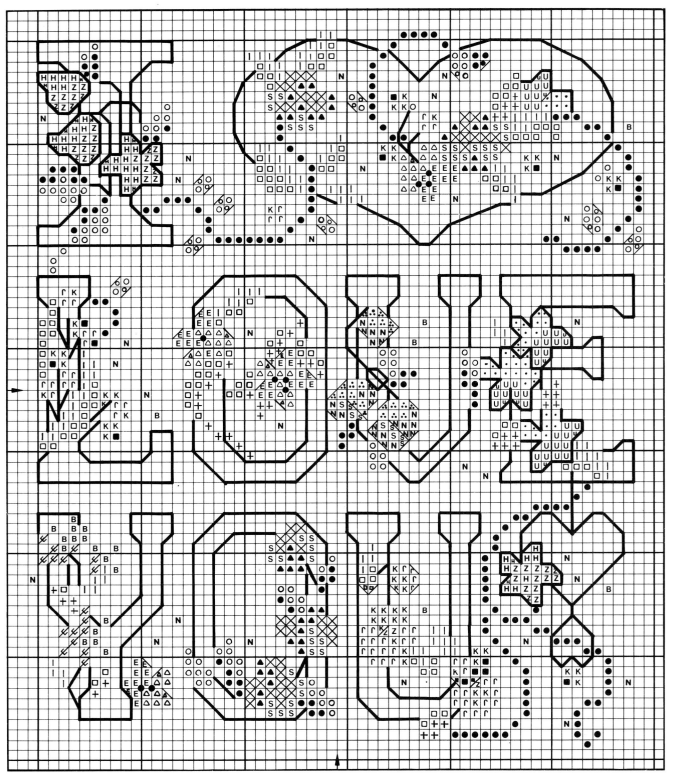

Stitch Count: 60 x 70

UDDERLY IN LOVE

SAMPLE

Stitched on Fiddler's Cloth 14, the finished design size is 6¼" x 4". (Adjust project measurements for other stitch counts.) The fabric was cut 11" x 9".

MATERIALS FOR CARD

Completed cross-stitch
One 7" x 5" piece of polyester fleece
8" length of ⅛"-wide brown satin ribbon
One ¾"-wide wooden heart
One 7" x 5" piece of lightweight cardboard

One 7" x 10" piece of medium-weight tan paper
Glue
Transparent tape
Dressmakers' pen
Tracing paper

DIRECTIONS

1. Complete Steps 1–4 of the cow card on pages 54–55.

2. Cut a 5½" length of ribbon and tie it into a 1½" bow. Glue the wooden heart 1½" below the top edge of cow (see photo). Glue one end of the remaining 2½" length of ribbon to the top of the heart and the other end to the back of the cow. Glue the bow over the heart.

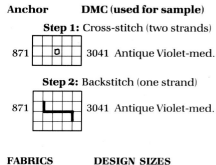

Anchor	DMC (used for sample)
Step 1: Cross-stitch (two strands)	
871	3041 Antique Violet-med.
Step 2: Backstitch (one strand)	
871	3041 Antique Violet-med.

FABRICS	DESIGN SIZES
Aida 11	3⅜" x 1¾"
Aida 14	2⅝" x 1⅜"
Aida 18	2" x 1⅛"
Hardanger 22	1⅝" x ⅞"

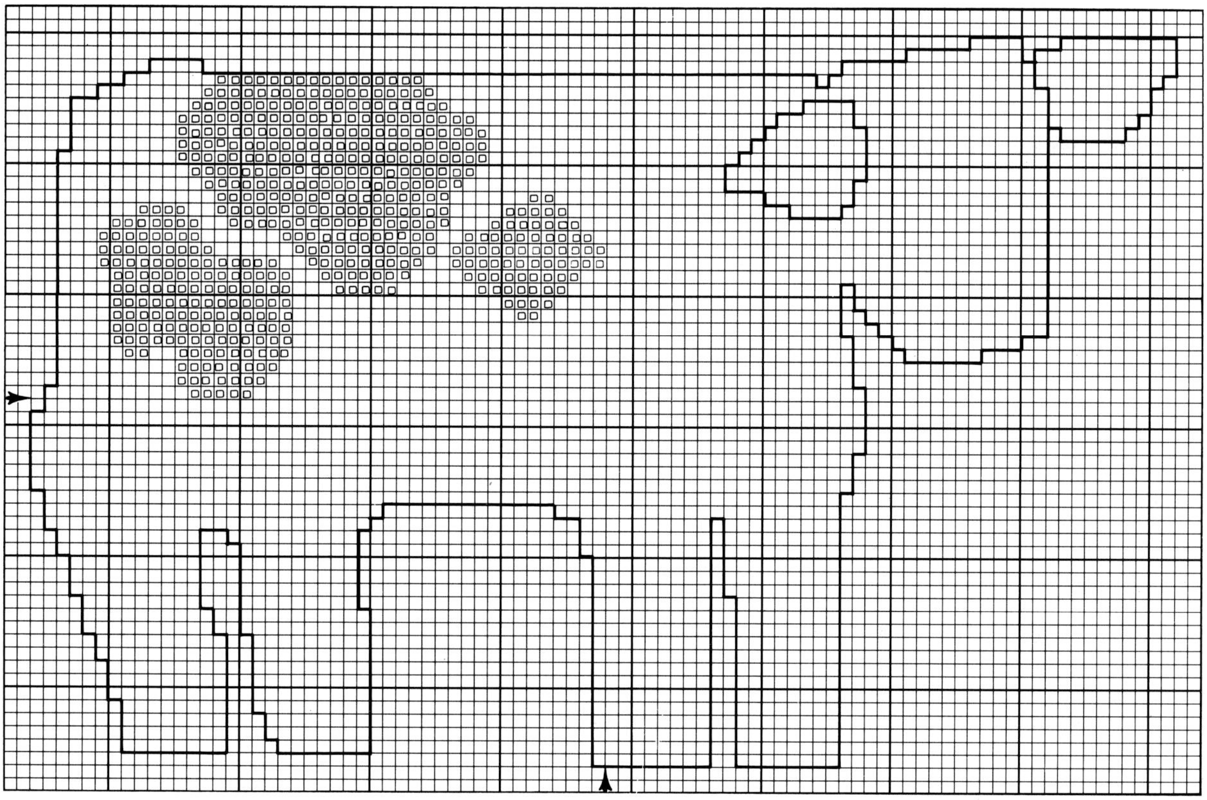

Stitch Count: 88 x 56

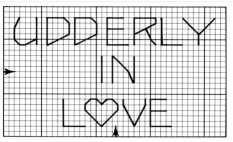

Stitch Count: 37 x 20

Anchor	DMC (used for sample)

Step 1: Backstitch (one strand)

871 | 3041 Antique Violet-med.

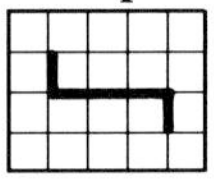

FABRICS	DESIGN SIZES
Aida 11	3⅜" x 1¾"
Aida 14	2⅝" x 1⅜"
Aida 18	2" x 1⅛"
Hardanger 22	1⅝" x ⅞"

SAMPLE

Stitched on Fiddler's Cloth 14, the finished design size is 2⅝" x 1⅜". (Adjust project measurements for other stitch counts.) The fabric was cut 6" x 6".

MATERIALS FOR COW

Completed cross-stitch
One 5" x 3½" piece of unstitched Fiddler's Cloth 14; matching thread
⅜ yard of 45"-wide mauve fabric; matching thread
Small pieces of tan fabric
1½ yards of ⅛"-wide mauve satin ribbon
Embroidery floss (DMC 3041 Antique Violet-med.)
Fusible web
Stuffing
Dressmakers' pen
Tracing paper

DIRECTIONS

All seam allowances are ¼".

1. Trace and cut out patterns on pages 58 and 59, adding ¼" seam allowances.

2. Cut two body pieces and four ear pieces from the mauve fabric. Cut three spots from the tan fabric. Cut three spots from the fusible web.

3. Fuse the spots to the front of the cow, according to manufacturer's directions. Buttonhole-stitch around each spot, using two strands of floss.

4. Complete Steps 4, 5, and 6 of the Christmas cow on page 56.

5. To make the cow's tail, cut three 10" lengths of ribbon. Knot the lengths together and braid.

Knot the second end and tack the tail to the body.

6. Center the heart pattern over the stitched design on the Fiddler's Cloth and cut out. Cut a heart piece for the back from the unstitched Fiddler's Cloth.

7. Pin the two heart pieces, right sides together and raw edges aligned. Stitch, leaving an opening for turning. Clip curves. Turn right side out and stuff firmly. Slipstitch the opening closed. Outline the heart with buttonhole stitch.

8. Cut the remaining ribbon into three equal lengths. Knot the lengths together at one end and make a 10" braid. Tie the two ends of the braid together. With the knot at the back of the cow's neck, tack the heart to the ribbon. Hang the heart around the cow's neck.

Home Sweet Home

FOR YOUR NEW HOME

WELCOME TO MY ROOST

Recipe: FOR MAKING A HOUSE A HOME
From: MARIE STEVENS   Serves: ONE FAMILY

Combine one husband and one wife;
And add for sheer delight,
Assorted children — any size
And mix with all your might.

Now add a pinch of helpfulness;

...Now add a pinch of helpfulness;
And loyalty galore
A dash of patience and a smile,
And faith — and stir some more.

Now sprinkle kindness over all,
For happiness and health,
Garnish it with love supreme,
And what you have is wealth.

Author Unknown

SAMPLE

Stitched on cream Aida 14, the finished design size is 4⅜" x 1⅜". (Adjust project measurements for other stitch counts.) The fabric was cut 8" x 6".

MATERIALS FOR CARD

Completed cross-stitch
Two ½" blue buttons
Fusible web
One 7" x 10" piece of medium-weight white paper
One 6" x 3" piece of lightweight blue paper
Glue

DIRECTIONS

1. Cut the Aida ¼" outside the design on all sides. Cut one piece of fusible web 4¾" x 1⅝". Center and fuse the design piece to the blue paper, according to manufacturer's directions.

2. Score the white paper in the center to make a 7" x 5" card.

3. Centering the blue paper horizontally and ½" below the folded edge, glue to the front of the card.

4. Glue the two buttons in place (see photo).

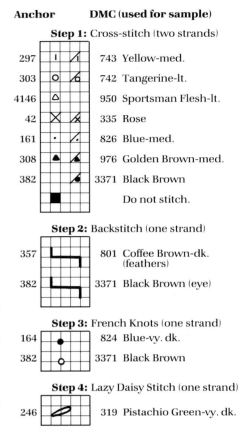

Anchor			DMC (used for sample)
Step 1: Cross-stitch (two strands)			
297	I	⁄	743 Yellow-med.
303	O	⁄	742 Tangerine-lt.
4146	△		950 Sportsman Flesh-lt.
42	X	⁄	335 Rose
161	·	⁄	826 Blue-med.
308	▲	⁄	976 Golden Brown-med.
382		⁄	3371 Black Brown
	■		Do not stitch.
Step 2: Backstitch (one strand)			
357			801 Coffee Brown-dk. (feathers)
382			3371 Black Brown (eye)
Step 3: French Knots (one strand)			
164	●		824 Blue-vy. dk.
382	○		3371 Black Brown
Step 4: Lazy Daisy Stitch (one strand)			
246	⟋		319 Pistachio Green-vy. dk.

FABRICS	DESIGN SIZES
Aida 11	5½" x 1¾"
Aida 18	3⅜" x 1⅛"
Hardanger 22	2¾" x ⅞"

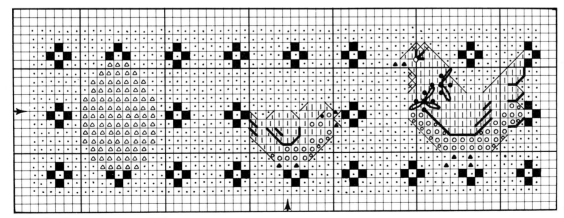

Stitch Count: 61 x 20

SAMPLE

Stitched on cream Aida 14, the finished design size is 5⅝" x 5⅝". (Adjust project measurements for other stitch counts.) The fabric was cut 12" x 12". (See Suppliers for buttons.)

MATERIALS FOR PICTURE

Completed cross-stitch
⅓ yard of 45"-wide tan print fabric
⅔ yard of 1/16"-wide red satin ribbon
Hen and chick buttons

Professionally cut mat
Glue
Masking tape
Pencil

DIRECTIONS

1. To ensure that the angles on the mat are square, have a professional framer cut the mat board. The outside edges are 10" x 10". The inside edges are 5⅝" x 5⅝".

2. To cover the mat, cut a 12" square from the tan fabric.

3. Place the fabric wrong side up on a flat surface. Center the mat on top of the fabric. Trace the inside edge, or window, of the mat. Make a second pencil line 2" inside this line. Cut along the inside pencil line. Clip the corners to the window outline at a 45° angle.

4. Reposition the mat on fabric, aligning window with the pencil line. Run a line of glue along the top outside edge of the mat to within 2" of the corners. Fold the fabric over the edge, making the surface taut. Tape. Repeat along the bottom edge, then the sides. Then glue along the window, beginning with the top inside edge.

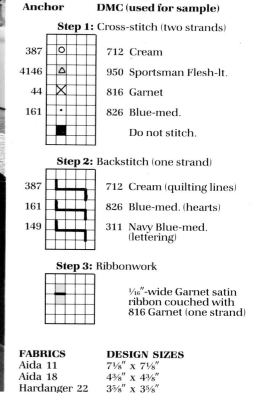

Anchor		DMC (used for sample)	
Step 1: Cross-stitch (two strands)			
387	O	712	Cream
4146	△	950	Sportsman Flesh-lt.
44	X	816	Garnet
161	·	826	Blue-med.
	■		Do not stitch.

Anchor		DMC	
Step 2: Backstitch (one strand)			
387		712	Cream (quilting lines)
161		826	Blue-med. (hearts)
149		311	Navy Blue-med. (lettering)

Step 3: Ribbonwork

1/16"-wide Garnet satin ribbon couched with 816 Garnet (one strand)

FABRICS	DESIGN SIZES
Aida 11	7⅛" x 7⅛"
Aida 18	4⅜" x 4⅜"
Hardanger 22	3⅝" x 3⅝"

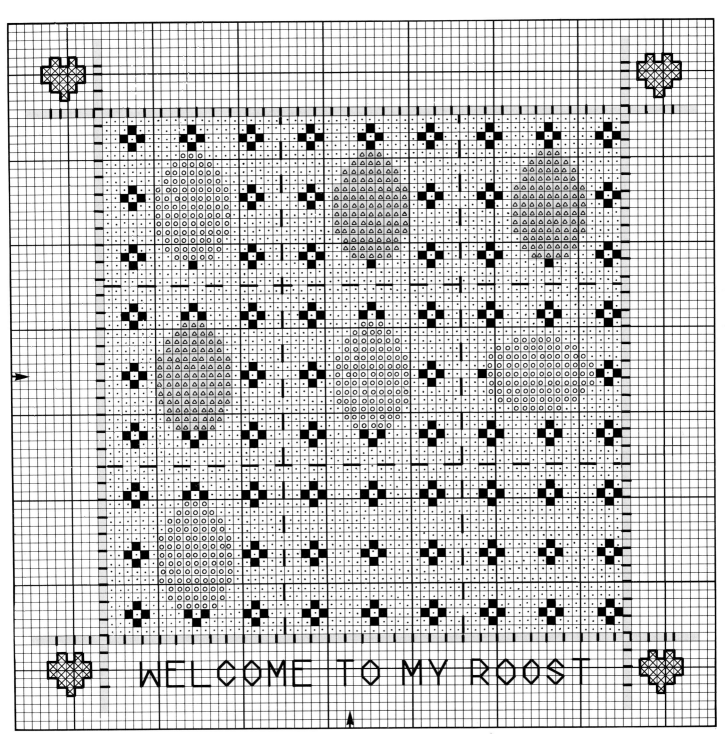

Stitch Count: 79 x 79

the mat to the front of the card, covering the ribbon ends. Leave ⅛" of white poster board showing around the outside of the blue mat.

For Your New Home

SAMPLE

Stitched on white Belfast Linen 32 over two threads, the finished design size is 4⅜" x 5½". (Adjust project measurements for other stitch counts.) Fabric was cut 8" x 10".

MATERIALS FOR CARD

Completed cross-stitch
1¼ yards of ⅛"-wide light blue satin ribbon; matching thread
⅞ yard of ⅛"-wide yellow satin ribbon; matching thread
Fusible web
One 16" x 9½" piece of white poster board
One 8" x 9¼" piece of blue mat board
Glue

DIRECTIONS

1. Cut the blue ribbon into two 8" lengths and four 7" lengths. Cut the yellow ribbon into two 8" lengths and two 7" lengths.

2. Arrange the blue ribbon pieces and yellow ribbon pieces and slip-stitch them to the cross-stitch piece as shown in the photograph.

3. Score the poster board in the center to make an 8" x 9½" card. Trim the design piece and fusible web to measure 7½" x 9". Center design piece on the front of the card and fuse in place according to manufacturer's directions.

4. From the back of the mat board, cut a 6" x 7½" window. Glue

Anchor			DMC (used for sample)
Step 1: Cross-stitch (two strands)			
1	·	╱	White
886	+	╱	3047 Yellow Beige-lt.
887	O	╱	3046 Yellow Beige-med.
892	I		225 Shell Pink-vy. lt.
893	□		224 Shell Pink-lt.
894	X		223 Shell Pink-med.
897	●	╱	221 Shell Pink-dk.
74	▲		3354 Dusty Rose-lt.
969	—		316 Antique Mauve-med.
869	∴		3042 Antique Violet-lt.
871	■		3041 Antique Violet-med.
858	△		524 Fern Green-vy. lt.
876	▢		502 Blue Green
842	·		3013 Khaki Green-lt.
844	O		3012 Khaki Green-med.
845	X		3011 Khaki Green-dk.
397	▽	╱	3072 Beaver Gray-vy. lt.

Step 2: Filet Cross-stitch (one strand)

920		932 Antique Blue-lt.

Step 3: Backstitch (one strand)

894		223 Shell Pink-med. (light pink flowers)
897		221 Shell Pink-dk. (dark pink flower)
921		931 Antique Blue-med. (white daisies)
845		3011 Khaki Green-dk. (all else)

FABRICS	DESIGN SIZES
Aida 11	6⅜" x 8⅛"
Aida 14	5" x 6⅜"
Aida 18	3⅞" x 5"
Hardanger 22	3⅛" x 4"

Stitch Count: 70 x 89

Stitched on toffee Oslo 22 over two threads, the finished design size is 9⅜" x 6⅛". (Adjust project measurements for other stitch counts.) The fabric was cut 15" x 11". To personalize, refer to the alphabet. Transfer the letters to graph paper; mark the center of the graph and begin stitching in the center of the space indicated.

MATERIALS FOR PILLOW

Completed cross-stitch
⅝ yard of 45"-wide rust print fabric; matching thread
½ yard of 45"-wide tan fabric; matching thread
¼ yard of 45"-wide cream fabric for cording; matching thread
1¼ yards of narrow cording
5 yards of ⅛"-wide rust ribbon
Dressmakers' pen
Stuffing

How sweet it is!

SAMPLE

Stitched on toffee Oslo 22 over two threads, the finished design size is 9⅜" x 3". (Adjust project measurements for other stitch counts.) Fabric was cut 12" x 6". Stitch lower half of design only.

MATERIALS FOR CARD

Completed cross-stitch
Fusible web
One 10¾" x 13½" piece of white poster board
One 10¾" x 4½" piece of blue watercolor paper
Cream thread
Glue

DIRECTIONS

1. Cut the Oslo 10¼" x 4⅛", with the design centered.

2. Fold under ¼" on all edges of the Oslo. Machine-stitch ⅛" from the folded edges, using the cream thread and the longest stitch.

3. Cut the fusible web 9¾" x 3⅝". Fuse the Oslo to the blue paper. Zigzag the edges of the Oslo through both layers.

4. Score the poster board in the center to make a 10¾" x 6¾" card. Glue the blue paper to the front of the card, ¼" below the score line.

DIRECTIONS

All seam allowances are ½".

1. Cut the Oslo 12½" x 9¼", with the design centered.

2. Cut one 12½" x 9¼" piece of rust fabric for the back. Also cut a 4"-wide bias strip, piecing as needed to equal 3¼ yards.

3. Cut a 5"-wide bias strip from the tan fabric, piecing as needed to equal 3¼ yards.

4. Cut a 1¼"-wide bias strip from the cream fabric, piecing as needed to equal 45". Cover the cording.

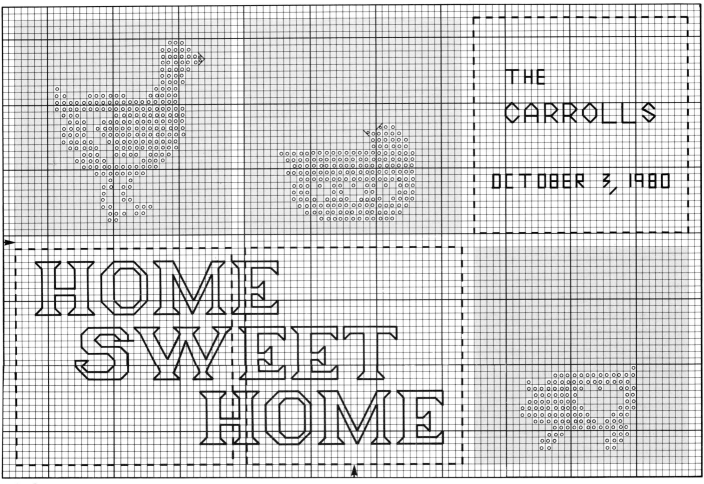

Stitch Count: 103 x 68

5. Stitch the cording to the right side of the pillow front, matching the raw edges and rounding the corners slightly.

6. With right sides together, stitch the ends of the rust bias strip together to form one continuous strip. With wrong sides together, fold the bias strip in half lengthwise; press. Divide the strip into quarters; mark the quarters on the raw edge. Repeat for the tan bias strip. Mark the center of each edge of the pillow front.

7. Stitch gathering threads through both layers of the rust strip, next to the raw edge. Gather. Repeat for the tan ruffle. Layer the pillow front, the print ruffle, and the tan ruffle, matching center marks. Pin ruffles in place, easing in fullness at corners. Stitch through all layers.

8. With ruffles toward the center of the pillow, pin the right sides of the pillow front and back together. Stitch on the stitching line of the ruffle, leaving a 4″ opening. Turn right side out and stuff. Slipstitch the opening closed.

9. Cut the ribbon into four equal lengths. Fold one length of ribbon into four 4″ loops. Knot the loops to form a bow. Tack the bow to one corner of the pillow. Repeat with the remaining lengths.

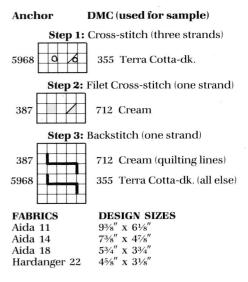

Anchor		DMC (used for sample)
Step 1:	Cross-stitch (three strands)	
5968		355 Terra Cotta-dk.
Step 2:	Filet Cross-stitch (one strand)	
387		712 Cream
Step 3:	Backstitch (one strand)	
387		712 Cream (quilting lines)
5968		355 Terra Cotta-dk. (all else)

FABRICS	DESIGN SIZES
Aida 11	9⅜″ x 6⅛″
Aida 14	7⅜″ x 4⅞″
Aida 18	5¾″ x 3¾″
Hardanger 22	4⅝″ x 3⅛″

SAMPLE

Stitched on cream Belfast Linen 32 over two threads. The finished design size of the heart is 3⅛" x 2¾"; the lettering is 2" x 1¾". (Adjust project measurements for other stitch counts.) The fabric was cut 17" x 11". Mark a 13½" x 8½" rectangle in the center of the fabric and see Diagram for placement of the stitching.

MATERIALS FOR LABEL

Completed cross-stitch; matching thread
One 13½" x 8½" piece of lightweight print fabric
Dressmakers' pen
Tracing paper
Cream double-fold bias tape

DIRECTIONS

1. Trace and cut out the pattern for the heart.

2. Cut the linen 13½" x 8½"; see Diagram for placement of the heart window in relation to the stitched design. Trace the heart onto the wrong side of the linen to make the window.

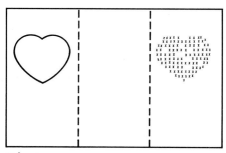

Diagram

3. Pin the linen and the lining, right sides together and raw edges aligned. Stitch only on the pen

Though time and space
May keep us apart
The memories we share
Have found places
in my heart.

Heart Pattern

line of the heart. Cut ¼″ inside the stitching line through both layers. Clip the curved seam allowance. Turn right side out and press.

4. Open the bias tape. Pin the right side of the bias tape to the right side of the linen, aligning raw edges. Stitch on the fold line of the bias tape. Fold the tape to the lining side; slipstitch.

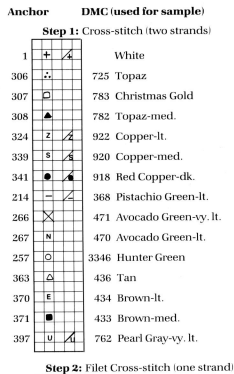

Anchor		DMC (used for sample)	
		Step 1: Cross-stitch (two strands)	
1	+ / ⁴	White	
306	∴	725	Topaz
307	◻	783	Christmas Gold
308	▲	782	Topaz-med.
324	Z / ⁴	922	Copper-lt.
339	S / ⁵	920	Copper-med.
341	● / ⁴	918	Red Copper-dk.
214	– / ⁄	368	Pistachio Green-lt.
266	✕	471	Avocado Green-vy. lt.
267	N	470	Avocado Green-lt.
257	O	3346	Hunter Green
363	△	436	Tan
370	E	434	Brown-lt.
371	▪	433	Brown-med.
397	U / ⁴	762	Pearl Gray-vy. lt.

Step 2: Filet Cross-stitch (one strand)

159	· / ⁄	827	Blue-vy. lt.

Heart

FABRICS	DESIGN SIZES
Aida 11	4½″ x 4″
Aida 14	3⅝″ x 3⅛″
Aida 18	2¾″ x 2½″
Hardanger 22	2¼″ x 2″

Lettering

FABRICS	DESIGN SIZES
Aida 11	2¾″ x 2½″
Aida 14	2¼″ x 2″
Aida 18	1¾″ x 1½″
Hardanger 22	1⅜″ x 1¼″

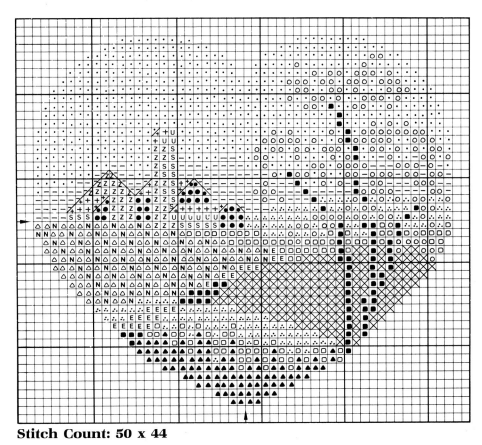

Stitch Count: 50 x 44

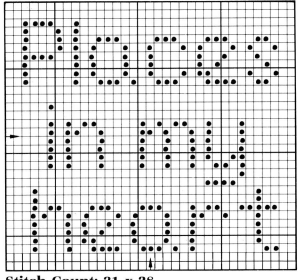

Stitch Count: 31 x 28

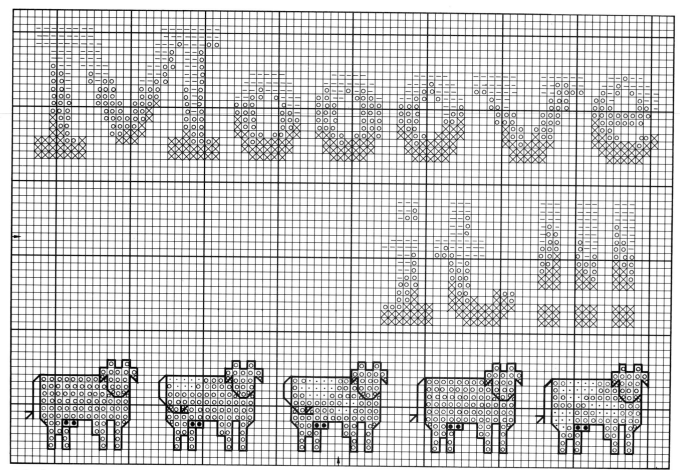

Stitch Count: 85 x 57

But come back and see us soon!

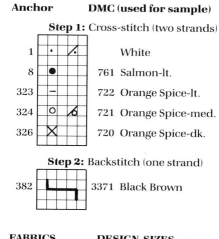

Cloud Patterns

SAMPLE

Stitched on brown Aida 14, the finished design size is 6⅛″ x 4⅛″. (Adjust project measurements for other stitch counts.) The fabric was cut 10″ x 8″.

MATERIALS FOR CARD

Completed cross-stitch
Fusible web
One 7½″ x 12″ piece of glossy white poster board
One 7½″ x 6″ piece of dark brown mat board
Small pieces of glossy white poster board
Rubber cement
Tracing paper

DIRECTIONS

1. Cut the Aida 6⅜″ x 4¾″, with the design centered. Cut one piece of fusible web 6⅜″ x 4¾″.

2. Center and fuse the Aida to the mat board, according to manufacturer's instructions.

3. Score the white poster board in the center to make a 7½″ x 6″ card. Glue the back of the mat board to the front of the card.

4. Trace the patterns for the clouds and cut out. Then trace the clouds onto small pieces of white poster board. Cut them out and glue them to the stitched design (see photo).

Anchor		DMC (used for sample)
Step 1: Cross-stitch (two strands)		
1		White
8		761 Salmon-lt.
323		722 Orange Spice-lt.
324		721 Orange Spice-med.
326		720 Orange Spice-dk.
Step 2: Backstitch (one strand)		
382		3371 Black Brown

FABRICS	DESIGN SIZES
Aida 11	7¾″ x 5⅛″
Aida 18	4¾″ x 3⅛″
Hardanger 22	3⅞″ x 2⅝″

SAMPLE

Stitched on brown Aida 14, the finished cross-stitch design size is 6″ x 2¾″. (Adjust project measurements for other stitch counts.) The fabric was cut 18″ x 12″. Omit the cows from the design, stitching only "Mooove it!!!" Before stitching, trace cow pattern onto the fabric; position stitching 2⅜″ from the left edge and 1½″ from the top edge.

MATERIALS FOR COW

Completed cross-stitch
One 16″ square of unstitched
  Aida 14; matching thread
9 yards of ¹⁄₁₆″-wide white satin
  ribbon

1½ yards of ⅛″-wide white satin
  ribbon
One 1″-wide brass bell
Large-eyed needle
Stuffing
Dressmakers' pen
Tracing paper

DIRECTIONS

All seam allowances are ¼″.

1. Trace and cut out patterns on pages 58–59, adding ¼″ seam allowances.

2. Center the pattern over the stitched design and trace the outline with the dressmakers' pen. Mark the placement for the spots.

3. To make the spots, thread a 25″ length of ¹⁄₁₆″-wide ribbon through the large-eyed needle. Following the outline of the spots, weave the ribbon through the Aida. For vertical rows of ribbon, bring the needle up at the bottom of the spot. Work your way across the spots, leaving two thread units of Aida between the rows of ribbon (Diagram). Tack ribbon ends to wrong side of Aida.

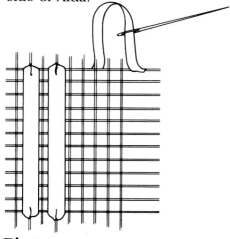

Diagram

4. Complete horizontal rows by weaving ribbon over and under vertical rows. Tack ribbon ends.

5. Complete Steps 2 through 6 for the cow on pages 56–57.

6. To make the cow's tail, cut three 10″ lengths of ribbon. Knot the lengths together and braid. Knot the second end and tack the tail to the body.

7. Cut the remaining ribbon into three equal lengths. Knot the lengths together at one end and make a 10″ braid. Slip the braid through the bell and tie the two ends of the braid together. Hang around the cow's neck.

Sympathy

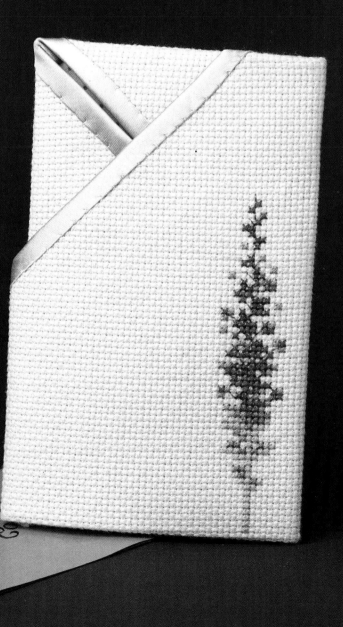

With deepest sympathy

SAMPLE

Stitched on light blue Aida 14, the finished design size is ¾" x 3⅞". (Adjust project measurements for other stitch counts.) The design was centered on the Aida, and the fabric was cut 14" x 14".

MATERIALS FOR ENVELOPE

Completed cross-stitch
One 7" x 10" piece of print fabric
1 yard of double-fold blue satin bias tape; matching thread
Fusible web
Dressmakers' pen

DIRECTIONS

1. Make a paper pattern and practice the folds before cutting the Aida. Mark the fold lines and cutting lines on the Aida with the dressmakers' pen. Cut carefully.

2. Cut the Aida 7" x 10" on the bias, using the lining for a pattern and referring to Diagram A for placement of the stitched design. Cut the fusible web 7" x 10".

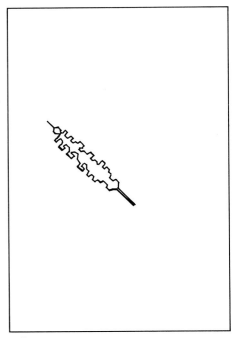

Diagram A

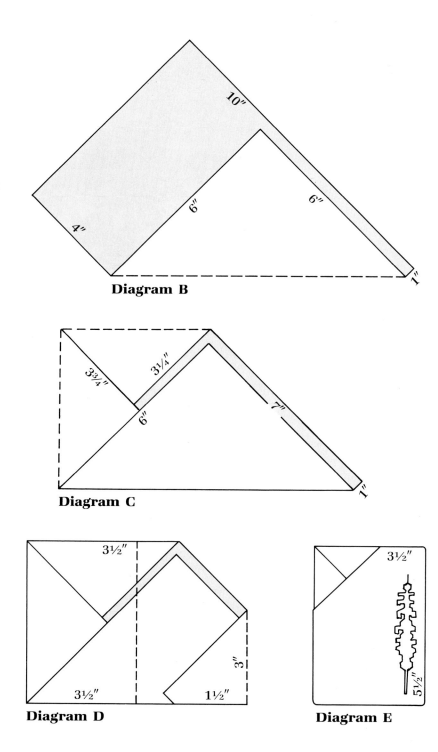

Diagram B

Diagram C

Diagram D

Diagram E

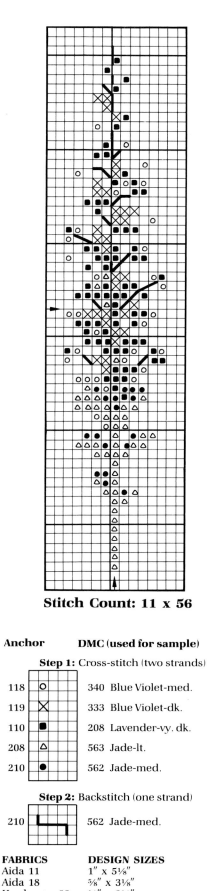

Stitch Count: 11 x 56

Anchor		DMC (used for sample)

Step 1: Cross-stitch (two strands)

118	O	340 Blue Violet-med.
119	X	333 Blue Violet-dk.
110	■	208 Lavender-vy. dk.
208	△	563 Jade-lt.
210	●	562 Jade-med.

Step 2: Backstitch (one strand)

| 210 | ⌐ | 562 Jade-med. |

FABRICS	DESIGN SIZES
Aida 11	1" x 5⅛"
Aida 18	⅝" x 3⅛"
Hardanger 22	½" x 2½"

3. Fuse the Aida to the lining, according to manufacturer's directions. Fold the bias tape in half and press. Encase the raw edges of the fabric in the bias tape. Machine-stitch through all layers, folding the corners of the bias tape at a 45° angle.

4. Fold the fabric (Diagrams B–E), pressing the folds with a hot iron.

Sympathy **99**

Where is the heart that doth not keep
Within its inmost core,
Some fond remembrance hidden deep
Of days that are no more.

Ellen C. Howarth

SAMPLE

Stitched on driftwood Belfast Linen 32 over two threads, finished design size is 3¼" x 2½". (Adjust project measurements for other stitch counts.) Fabric was cut 15" x 15". Design is centered horizontally, with the bottom corner 2½" from edge of fabric.

MATERIALS FOR ENVELOPE

Completed cross-stitch
One 10" square of tan fabric
1 yard of ½"-wide cream rayon seam binding; matching thread
Fusible web
Dressmakers' pen
Tracing paper

DIRECTIONS

1. Make a pattern for an 8" square. Place the pattern over the linen with one corner in the center of the stitched design, noting the straight of the grain of the fabric (Diagram A). Trace around the square with the dressmakers' pen.

2. Cut the fusible web to match the linen. Following the manufacturer's directions, fuse the wrong side of the linen to the tan fabric, making sure that the fabric extends to the edge of flower design.

3. Using a narrow satin stitch, machine-stitch around the part of the design extending beyond the pen lines. Be careful not to stitch into the design. Trim the lining even with the linen, cutting very close to the satin stitching around the stitched design.

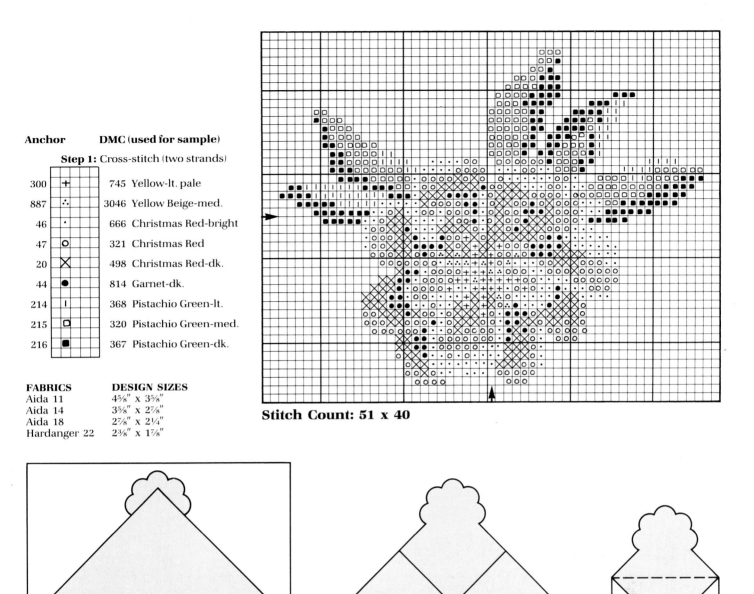

Anchor   **DMC (used for sample)**

Step 1: Cross-stitch (two strands)

Anchor		DMC	
300	+	745	Yellow-lt. pale
887	∴	3046	Yellow Beige-med.
46	·	666	Christmas Red-bright
47	O	321	Christmas Red
20	X	498	Christmas Red-dk.
44	●	814	Garnet-dk.
214	I	368	Pistachio Green-lt.
215	□	320	Pistachio Green-med.
216	■	367	Pistachio Green-dk.

FABRICS	DESIGN SIZES
Aida 11	4⅝" x 3⅝"
Aida 14	3⅝" x 2⅞"
Aida 18	2⅞" x 2¼"
Hardanger 22	2⅜" x 1⅞"

Stitch Count: 51 x 40

Diagram A

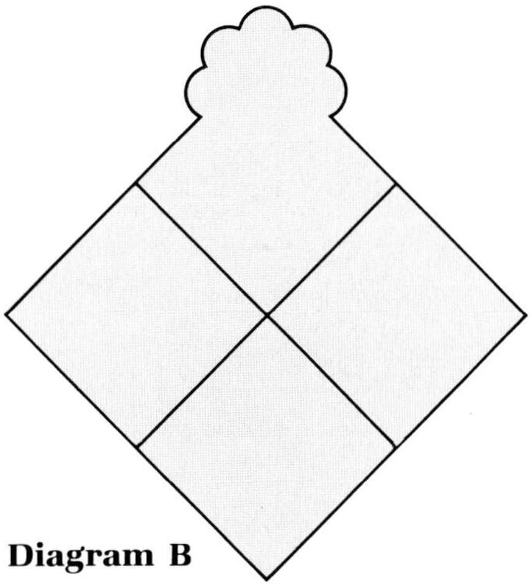

Diagram B

Diagram C

4. Fold the rayon binding in half and press. Encase the straight edges of the fabric in the binding. Machine-stitch through all layers, folding the corners of the binding at a 45° angle.

5. Mark the centers of the 8" edges with the dressmakers' pen.

Draw a line from the center of one edge to the center of the opposite edge. Repeat for the remaining edges (Diagram B).

6. Fold three corners to meet at the center (Diagram B). Press the folds. Slipstitch the lower edges together to make an envelope

(Diagram C). Fold the design to the center, covering the other corners. Press the fold.

Sympathy **101**

Our Cares Behind, Our Hopes Ahead

1. Complete all the steps for the envelope shown on page 100–101.

SAMPLE

Stitched on cream Belfast Linen 32 over two threads, the finished design size is 3⅛" x 2½". (Adjust project measurements for other stitch counts.) The fabric was cut 15" x 15". Position the stitching so that the design is centered horizontally, 2½" from the bottom edge of the fabric.

MATERIALS FOR ENVELOPE

Completed cross-stitch
One 10" square of pink light-weight fabric
1 yard of ½"-wide cream rayon seam binding; matching thread
Fusible web
Dressmakers' pen
Tracing paper

DIRECTIONS

1. Complete all the steps for the envelope shown on page 100–101.

Anchor		DMC (used for sample)
	Step 1: Cross-stitch (two strands)	
300	∴	745 Yellow-lt. pale
778	•	754 Peach Flesh-lt.
8	−	761 Salmon-lt.
9	O	760 Salmon
11	X	3328 Salmon-med.
13	▲	347 Salmon-dk.
214	+	368 Pistachio Green-lt.
215	□	320 Pistachio Green-med.
216	■	367 Pistachio Green-dk.

FABRICS	DESIGN SIZES
Aida 11	4½" x 3½"
Aida 14	3⅝" x 2¾"
Aida 18	2¾" x 2⅛"
Hardanger 22	2¼" x 1¾"

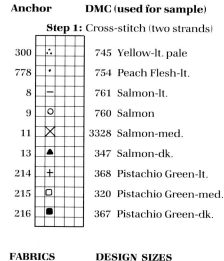

Stitch Count: 50 x 39

Holidays

Be My
Valentine

Heart Pattern

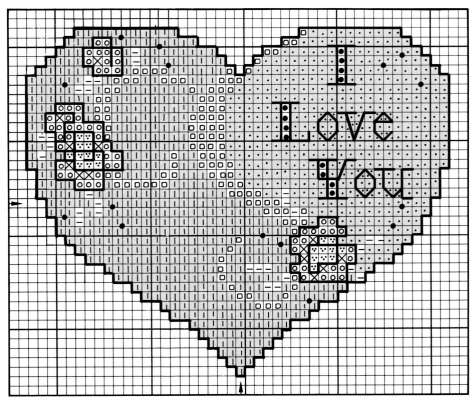

Stitch Count: 45 x 37

SAMPLE

Stitched on cream Belfast Linen 32 over two threads, the finished design size is 2¾″ x 2¼″. (Adjust project measurements for other stitch counts.) The fabric was cut 6″ x 6″.

MATERIALS FOR CARD

Completed cross-stitch; matching thread
One 11″ x 9″ piece of gray pindot fabric
One 4½″ square of muslin
1 yard of ¹⁄₁₆″-wide blue rayon braid; matching thread
Small amount of stuffing
Fusible web
One 11″ x 7″ piece of medium-weight white paper
One 10¾″ x 6¾″ piece of lightweight gray paper
Dressmakers' pen
Tracing paper
Rubber cement

DIRECTIONS

1. Pin the muslin to the wrong side of the linen, behind the design. Using matching thread, sew a small running stitch through both layers, very close to the edge of the design. Cut a slash in the muslin only and stuff the heart lightly. Whipstitch the slash closed.

2. Tack the rayon braid to the linen, ⅛″ outside the design, leaving ends of equal length. Tie the ends in a bow.

3. Trace and cut out the pattern for the heart. Center the pattern over the stitched design and trace with the dressmakers' pen. Cut

through both layers of fabric, ¼″ outside the pen lines. Clip the curved seam allowance.

4. Folding under the ¼″ seam allowance, slipstitch the heart to the gray fabric (see photo).

5. Score the white paper in the center to make a 5½″ x 7″ card. Cut a piece of fusible web 11″ x 9″. Following manufacturer's directions, center and fuse the gray fabric to the outside surface of the card, wrapping the excess fabric to the inside along the top and bottom edges.

6. Fold the gray paper to measure 5⅜″ x 6¾″. Place it inside the card, matching the fold line to the score line. Tack with rubber cement along the score line and on the corners to hide the raw edges of the gray fabric.

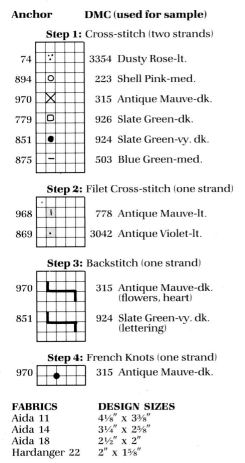

Anchor		DMC (used for sample)
Step 1: Cross-stitch (two strands)		
74	∵	3354 Dusty Rose-lt.
894	O	223 Shell Pink-med.
970	X	315 Antique Mauve-dk.
779	□	926 Slate Green-dk.
851	●	924 Slate Green-vy. dk.
875	−	503 Blue Green-med.
Step 2: Filet Cross-stitch (one strand)		
968	˴	778 Antique Mauve-lt.
869	·	3042 Antique Violet-lt.
Step 3: Backstitch (one strand)		
970		315 Antique Mauve-dk. (flowers, heart)
851		924 Slate Green-vy. dk. (lettering)
Step 4: French Knots (one strand)		
970	●	315 Antique Mauve-dk.

FABRICS	DESIGN SIZES
Aida 11	4⅛″ x 3⅜″
Aida 14	3¼″ x 2⅝″
Aida 18	2½″ x 2″
Hardanger 22	2″ x 1⅝″

Happy Valentine's Day

SAMPLE

Stitched on white Belfast Linen 32 over two threads, the finished design size is 4" x 3¼". (Adjust project measurements for other stitch counts.) The fabric was cut 9" x 8".

MATERIALS FOR CARD

Completed cross-stitch; matching thread
1 yard of ¹⁄₁₆"-wide purple rayon braid

Fusible web
One 8" x 14" piece of medium-weight white paper
One 7¾" x 6¾" piece of light-weight gray paper
Rubber cement

DIRECTIONS

1. Cut the linen 7" x 6", with the design centered. Cut one piece of fusible web 7" x 6".

2. Score the white paper in the center to make an 8" x 7" card. Center and fuse the linen to the front of the card, according to manufacturer's instructions.

3. Mark a 4¾" x 3¾" window on the back of the gray paper. Cut the window to make the mat. Using white thread and the longest stitch, machine-stitch on the gray paper in parallel rows, ¼" and ½" outside the edge of the window.

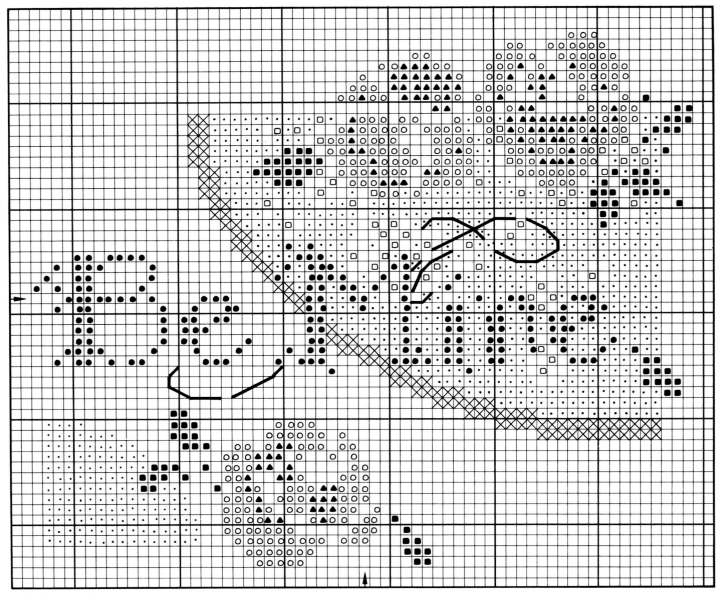

Stitch Count: 63 x 51

4. Place the braid between the rows of stitching, beginning 2½″ from the left edge of the mat. Set the machine to the widest zigzag stitch and zigzag over the braid, attaching it to the gray paper. Allow 8″ of the braid to hang loose on each end.

5. Tie the loose braid in a bow. Knot the ends and trim.

6. Center and glue the mat over the design, allowing ⅛″ of the card to show around outside edges.

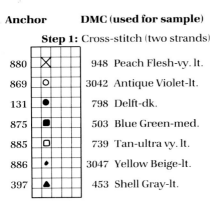

Anchor		DMC (used for sample)	
		Step 1: Cross-stitch (two strands)	
880	X	948	Peach Flesh-vy. lt.
869	O	3042	Antique Violet-lt.
131	●	798	Delft-dk.
875	■	503	Blue Green-med.
885	□	739	Tan-ultra vy. lt.
886	•	3047	Yellow Beige-lt.
397	▲	453	Shell Gray-lt.

Step 2: Backstitch (one strand)

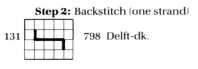

131 798 Delft-dk.

FABRICS	DESIGN SIZES
Aida 11	5¾″ x 4⅝″
Aida 14	4½″ x 3⅝″
Aida 18	3½″ x 2⅞″
Hardanger 22	2⅞″ x 2⅜″

Alleluia

SAMPLE

Stitched on white Linda 27 over two threads, the finished design size is 5⅛" x 3¾". (Adjust project measurements for other stitch counts.) Fabric was cut 10" x 8".

MATERIALS FOR CARD

Completed cross-stitch; matching thread
One 7" x 5¾" piece of light green fabric; matching thread
¾ yard of double-fold blue satin bias tape; matching thread
Fusible web
One 7¼" x 12½" piece of medium-weight glossy white paper
Dressmakers' pen

Anchor			DMC (used for sample)	
Step 1: Cross-stitch (two strands)				
1	·	⁄	White	
300	∴		745	Yellow-lt. pale
301	o	⁄	744	Yellow-pale
297	●	⁄	743	Yellow-med.
158			747	Sky Blue-vy. lt.
213	l		369	Pistachio Green-vy. lt.
214	o		368	Pistachio Green-lt.
215	X	⁄	320	Pistachio Green-med.
397	−	⁄	762	Pearl Gray-vy. lt.
398	X	⁄	415	Pearl Gray

Anchor		DMC (used for sample)	
Step 2: Backstitch (one strand)			
300		745	Yellow-lt. pale (corners)
215		320	Pistachio Green-med. (lettering, border, stems)
309		435	Brown-vy. lt. (flowers)
400		414	Steel Gray-dk. (birds)

Anchor		DMC (used for sample)	
Step 3: French Knots (one strand)			
215	○	320	Pistachio Green-med.
400	●	414	Steel Gray-dk.

FABRICS	DESIGN SIZES
Aida 11	6⅞" x 5¼"
Aida 14	5⅜" x 4⅛"
Aida 18	4⅛" x 3¼"
Hardanger 22	3⅜" x 2⅝"

Stitch Count: 75 x 58

DIRECTIONS

1. Cut the Linda 5½″ x 4¼″, with the design centered. Cut one piece of fusible web 5½″ x 4¼″ and one piece 7″ x 5¾″.

2. Center and fuse the Linda to the green fabric. Using white thread, machine-satin-stitch the edge of the Linda. Encase the raw edges of the green fabric in the bias tape. Machine-stitch through all layers, folding the corners at a 45° angle.

3. Using the dressmakers' pen, mark the scallops on the green fabric in the space between the Linda and the binding (see photo). With green thread, machine-stitch the scallops.

4. Score the paper in the center to make a 7¼″ x 6¼″ card. Center the Linda horizontally on the front of the card, aligning the top edge of the Linda with the fold at the top of the card. Fuse the design piece to the card, according to manufacturer's instructions.

Easter Greetings

SAMPLE

Stitched on light blue Aida 14, the finished design size is 3¾" x 3¾". (Adjust project measurements for other stitch counts.) The fabric was cut 7" x 7".

MATERIALS FOR CARD

Completed cross-stitch
One 3½" square of polyester fleece
Fusible web
One 5" x 11" piece of medium-weight white paper
One 5" x 5½" piece of light-weight white paper
Rubber cement

DIRECTIONS

1. Cut the Aida 5" x 5½", with the lower edge of the design 1¼" from the edge of the fabric. Cut the fusible web 5" x 5½".

2. Center and pin the fleece to the wrong side of the design; baste.

3. Place the Aida over the lightweight paper. Fuse the edges outside of the design area to the paper, according to manufacturer's directions. Trim the Aida and the lightweight paper ½" outside the design on the tops and sides and 1" outside the design on the bottoms.

4. Score the medium-weight white paper in the center to make a 5" x 5½" card. Glue the design to the center front of the card.

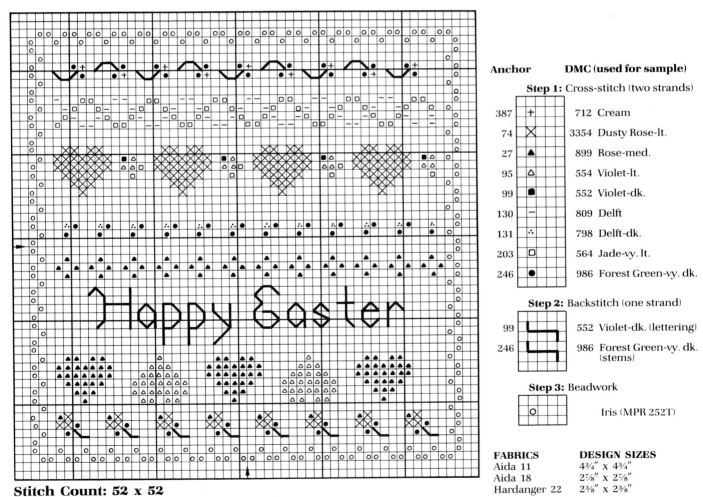

Stitch Count: 52 x 52

Anchor		DMC (used for sample)
Step 1: Cross-stitch (two strands)		
387	+	712 Cream
74	X	3354 Dusty Rose-lt.
27	▲	899 Rose-med.
95	△	554 Violet-lt.
99	■	552 Violet-dk.
130	–	809 Delft
131	∴	798 Delft-dk.
203	□	564 Jade-vy. lt.
246	●	986 Forest Green-vy. dk.
Step 2: Backstitch (one strand)		
99		552 Violet-dk. (lettering)
246		986 Forest Green-vy. dk. (stems)
Step 3: Beadwork		
	O	Iris (MPR 252T)

FABRICS	DESIGN SIZES
Aida 11	4¾" x 4¾"
Aida 18	2⅞" x 2⅞"
Hardanger 22	2⅜" x 2⅜"

SAMPLE

Stitched on light blue Aida 14, the finished design is 3¾" x 3¾". (Adjust project measurements for other stitch counts.) The fabric was cut 7" x 7".

MATERIALS FOR PILLOW

Completed cross-stitch
¼ yard of 45"-wide light blue fabric; matching thread
1½ yards of ⅜"-wide light blue satin ribbon
¾ yard of medium cording
Stuffing

DIRECTIONS

All seam allowances are ¼".

1. Cut the Aida in a 5" square, with the design centered.

2. Cut one 5" square from the blue fabric for the back. Also cut a 1"-wide bias strip, piecing as needed to equal 24". Cover cording.

3. Aligning raw edges, stitch the cording to the right side of the pillow.

4. Pin the front piece to the back piece, right sides together and raw edges aligned. Stitch along the stitching line of the cording, leaving a 3" opening in the bottom edge for turning. Clip the corners and turn right side out.

5. Insert stuffing until firm. Slipstitch the opening closed.

6. Cut one 30" and two 10" lengths of ribbon. Fold one end of the 30"

length into loops (see Diagram) and tack to the front of the pillow. Repeat at the other end of the 30" length. Tie each 10" length in a 2" bow. Tack the bows to the pillow (see photo). Trim the ribbon ends.

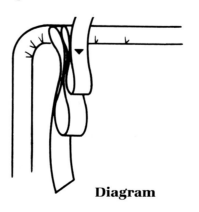

Diagram

SAMPLE

Stitched on light blue Aida 14, the finished design size is 3¾" x 3¾". (Adjust project measurements for other stitch counts.) The fabric was cut 7" x 7". (See Suppliers for information on ordering beads and buttons.)

MATERIALS FOR MUSIC BOX

Completed cross-stitch
¼ yard of 45"-wide light blue fabric; matching thread
Small piece of rose-colored fabric; matching floss

½ yard of ⅜"-wide light blue
    satin ribbon
¾ yard of medium cording
Stuffing
Two rabbit buttons
Graphite paper
Small music box

DIRECTIONS

All seam allowances are ¼".

1. Cut the Aida in a 5" square,
with the design centered.

2. Trace and cut out the heart
pattern, adding ¼" seam allowance. Trace the heart onto rose
fabric and cut out. Using graphite
paper, transfer markings. Embroi-
der flower petals and leaves, using
a lazy daisy stitch. Chain-stitch
the stem. Make a French knot in
the center of the flower. Make remaining French knots as shown
on the pattern. Buttonhole-stitch
the heart to the Aida (see photo).
Sew on rabbit buttons.

3. Follow Steps 2–3 for pillow.

4. Make a buttonhole in the center of the back piece. The hole
should be large enough to fit
around the key of the music box.

5. Follow Step 4 for pillow.

6. Insert a small amount of stuffing in the corners and across the
top. Insert the music box, placing
the key through the buttonhole.
Fill in around the music box with
stuffing until firm. Slipstitch the
opening closed.

7. Follow Step 6 for pillow.

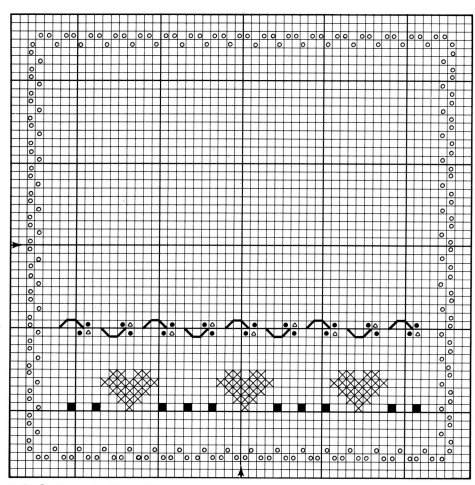

Stitch Count: 52 x 52

Anchor		DMC (used for sample)
	Step 1:	Cross-stitch (two strands)
74	✕	3354 Dusty Rose-lt.
95	△	554 Violet-lt.
246	●	986 Forest Green-vy. dk.
	Step 2:	Backstitch (one strand)
246	⌐	986 Forest Green-vy. dk.
	Step 3:	Beadwork
	■	Sapphire (MPR 168T)
	○	Emerald (MPR 332)

FABRICS	DESIGN SIZES
Aida 11	4¾" x 4¾"
Aida 18	2⅞" x 2⅞"
Hardanger 22	2⅜" x 2⅜"

Heart Pattern

Happy Mother's Day

Anchor			DMC (used for sample)	
Step 1: Cross-stitch (two strands)				
292	·	╱	3078	Golden Yellow-vy. lt.
886	▽	◸	3047	Yellow Beige-lt.
366	·	╱	951	Sportsman Flesh-vy. lt.
4146	+	◿	950	Sportsman Flesh-lt.
74	∴	◹	3354	Dusty Rose-lt.
42	O	◢	3350	Dusty Rose-vy. dk.
897	●	◤	221	Shell Pink-dk.
871	■		3041	Antique Violet-med.
120	I		794	Cornflower Blue-lt.
121	☐		793	Cornflower Blue-med.
147	▲		312	Navy Blue-lt.
206	△		955	Nile Green-lt.
214	−		368	Pistachio Green-lt.
215	☐		320	Pistachio Green-med.
246	✕		319	Pistachio Green-vy. dk.
378	▨	╱	841	Beige Brown-lt.
371	O	◢	433	Brown-med.
360	∵	◿	898	Coffee Brown-vy. dk.

Step 2: Backstitch (one strand)

42	⌐_	3350	Dusty Rose-vy. dk. (bottom row of lettering)
897	⌐_	221	Shell Pink-dk. (top row of lettering)
401	⌐_	844	Beaver Gray-ultra dk. (all else)

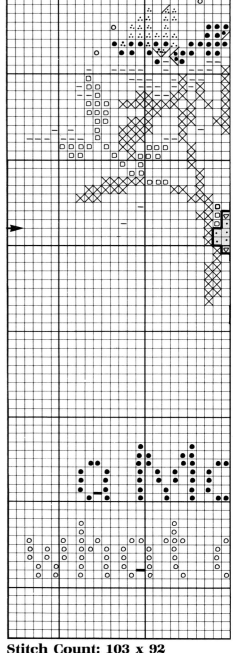

Stitch Count: 103 x 92

SAMPLE

Stitched on white Aida 14, the finished design size is 7⅜″ x 6⅝″. (Adjust project measurements for other stitch counts.) The fabric was cut 12″ x 11″.

FABRICS	DESIGN SIZES
Aida 11	9⅜″ x 8⅜″
Aida 18	5¾″ x 5⅛″
Hardanger 22	4⅝″ x 4⅛″

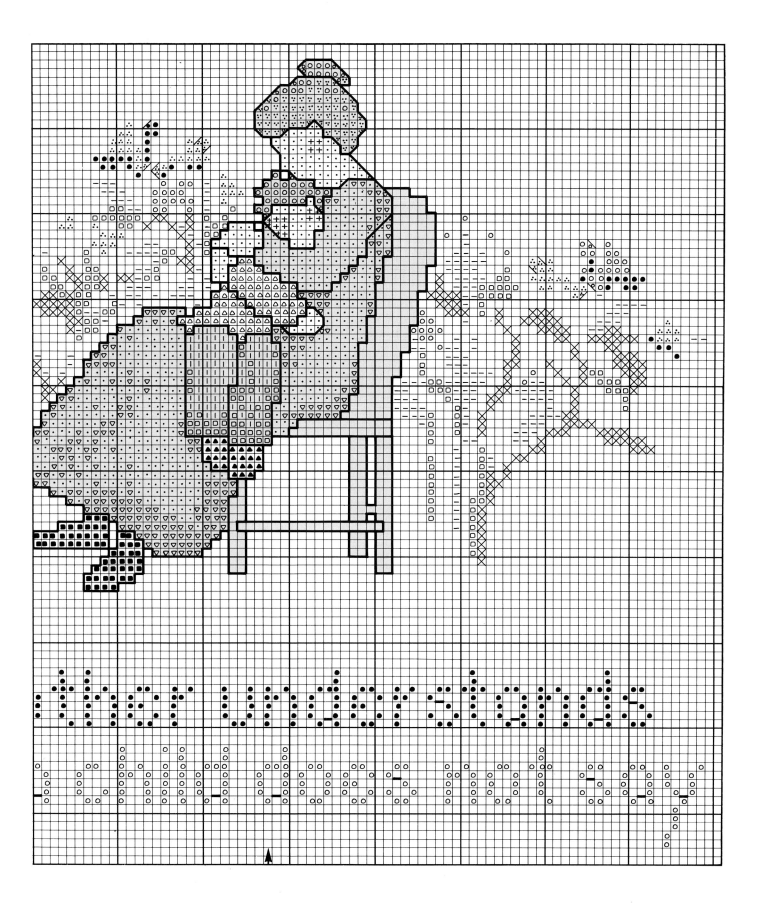

MATERIALS FOR CARD

Completed cross-stitch; matching thread
One 11″ x 20½″ piece of white poster board
One 11″ x 10¼″ piece of gray watercolor paper
One 11″ x 10¼″ piece of green watercolor paper
Fusible web
Rubber cement
Tracing paper

DIRECTIONS

1. Cut the Aida 10¾″ x 10″, with the design centered horizontally and the stitching placed 2″ above the bottom edge of the Aida. Cut a piece of fusible web 10¾″ x 10″.

2. Trace and cut out the pattern for the window in both sizes. Place the larger window pattern on the back of the gray paper, centered horizontally and 1⅝″ above an 11″ edge. Trace the pattern and cut out the window to make the mat.

3. Repeat Step 2 with the smaller pattern on the green paper. Position the pattern 2″ above an 11″ edge. Cut out the window to make the mat.

4. Using white thread and the longest stitch, machine-stitch ⅛″ outside window on green mat.

5. Center the mats and glue them together.

6. Score the poster board in the center to make an 11″ x 10¼″ card. Center the stitched design horizontally and 2¼″ above the bottom 11″ edge. Fuse the Aida to the front of the card, according to manufacturer's directions. Center and glue the mats to the front of the card.

Window Pattern

I love you with all of my hearts.

SAMPLE

Stitched on cream Belfast Linen 32 over two threads, the finished design size is 1¾" x 2". (Adjust project measurements for other stitch counts.) The fabric was cut 6" x 6".

MATERIALS FOR CARD

Completed cross-stitch
Fusible web
One 4½" x 10½" piece of
    medium-weight white paper
One 4" x 4⅜" piece of medium-
    weight cream paper
Rubber cement

DIRECTIONS

1. Cut the linen 2¾" x 3", with the design centered. Cut the fusible web 2¾" x 3".

2. Score the white paper in the center to make a 4½" x 5¼" card. Center the design piece horizontally, with the top of the design 1⅜" from the score line. Fuse the linen to the card front, according to manufacturer's directions.

3. Mark a 2" x 2¼" window on the back of the cream paper. Cut out the window to make the mat. Center the mat over the stitched design and glue it to the card front.

Anchor		DMC (used for sample)
Step 1: Cross-stitch (two strands)		
893	–	224 Shell Pink-lt.
894	▢	223 Shell Pink-med.
970	▼	315 Antique Mauve-dk.
871	✕	3041 Antique Violet-med.
921	○	931 Antique Blue-med.
876	◼	502 Blue Green

FABRICS	DESIGN SIZES
Aida 11	2½" x 2⅞"
Aida 14	1⅞" x 2¼"
Aida 18	1½" x 1¾"
Hardanger 22	1¼" x 1½"

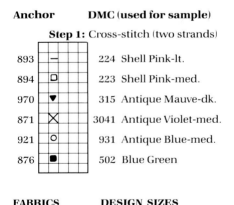

Stitch Count: 27 x 32

happy father's day!

SAMPLE

Stitched on gray Glenshee Linen 29 over two threads, the finished design size is 3⅜" x 1¼". (Adjust project measurements for other stitch counts.) The fabric was cut 8" x 6".

MATERIALS FOR CARD

Completed cross-stitch; matching thread
One 8½" x 6" piece of white watercolor paper
Colored pencils: dark blue, purple
White glue
Tracing paper
One small piece of graphite paper

DIRECTIONS

All seam allowances are ¼".

1. Cut the linen for the tie 4" x 3", with the design centered. Cut the linen for the band 1½" x 2¼", with the design centered.

2. With right sides together, fold the tie in half so that the 4" edges meet. Stitch along the 4" edge. Refold the tie so that the seam is across the center back. Stitch one end of the tie and then turn right side out. Fold ¼" inside at the open end. Slipstitch the opening closed.

3. Repeat Step 2 for the band, stitching the 2¼" sides together first. Wrap the band around the center of the tie tightly enough to form a tuck in the tie. Slipstitch the ends of the band together. Set the tie aside.

4. Score the watercolor paper in the center to make a 4¼″ x 6″ card.

5. Trace and cut out the pattern for the shirt. Using the piece of graphite paper, trace the pattern onto the front of the card and transfer all markings. Cut out the neck. Draw the collar, center front line, and buttons with the dark blue pencil. Using the side of the dark blue pencil, shade the shirt front very lightly. Draw the stripes, using the purple pencil.

6. Glue the bow tie to the front of the card.

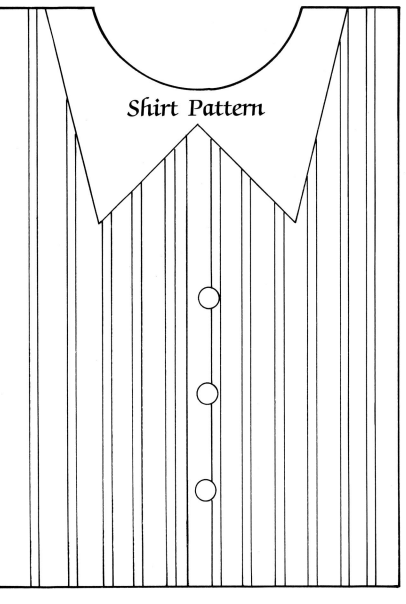

Shirt Pattern

Anchor   DMC (used for sample)

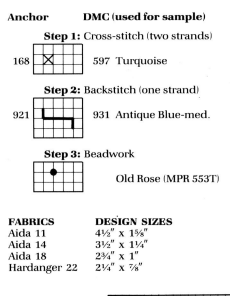

Step 1: Cross-stitch (two strands)

168 ⊠ 597 Turquoise

Step 2: Backstitch (one strand)

921 597 931 Antique Blue-med.

Step 3: Beadwork

• Old Rose (MPR 553T)

FABRICS   **DESIGN SIZES**
Aida 11   4½″ x 1⅝″
Aida 14   3½″ x 1¼″
Aida 18   2¾″ x 1″
Hardanger 22   2¼″ x ⅞″

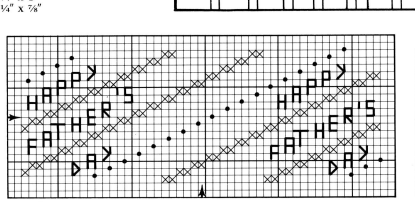

Stitch Count: 49 x 18

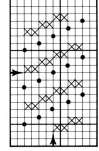

Stitch Count: 8 x 15

The year grows rich as it groweth old,
And life's latest sands are the sands of gold.

Julia C. R. Dorr

SAMPLE

Stitched on white Linda 27 over two threads, the finished design size is 6½" x 3⅛". (Adjust project measurements for other stitch counts.) Fabric was cut 11" x 7".

MATERIALS

Completed cross-stitch
One 10" x 6" piece of tan fabric; matching thread
Fusible web

One 10" x 12" piece of medium-weight cream paper
One 10" x 6" piece of medium-weight cream paper
Rubber cement
Dressmakers' pen

DIRECTIONS

1. Using the dressmakers' pen, mark a 7¼″ x 3¼″ window on the tan fabric. Cut ¼″ inside the pen line. Clip the corners. Fold the ¼″ seam allowance to the wrong side of the fabric; press. Place the window over the stitched design, with the design centered horizontally and ½″ above the tan fabric. Slipstitch the tan fabric to the Linda. Trim the Linda ¼″ on all edges.

2. Score the 10″ x 12″ piece of paper in the center to make a 10″ x 6″ card.

3. Trim the tan fabric to measure 9½″ x 5½″. Cut the fusible web 9½″ x 5½″. Center and fuse the Linda and tan fabric to the front of the card, according to manufacturer's instructions.

4. Mark an 8½″ x 4½″ window on the back of the 10″ x 6″ piece of paper. Cut the window to make a mat. Glue the mat to the front of the card, sealing the edges of the mat to the card front.

Anchor		DMC (used for sample)
Step 1: Cross-stitch (two strands)		
880	·	948 Peach Flesh-vy. lt.
868	□	758 Terra Cotta-lt.
347	△	402 Mahogany-vy. lt.
324	⊙	922 Copper-lt.
339	▲	920 Copper-med.
5975	●	356 Terra Cotta-med.
871	■	3041 Antique Violet-med.
158	+	747 Sky Blue-vy. lt.
167	∴	519 Sky Blue
213	−	504 Blue Green-lt.

Anchor		DMC
186	O	993 Aquamarine-lt.
189	X	991 Aquamarine-dk.
891	X	676 Old Gold-lt.
362	I	437 Tan-lt.
309		435 Brown-vy. lt.
Step 2: Backstitch (one strand)		
357	⌐	801 Coffee Brown-dk.
Step 3: French Knots (one strand)		
357	●	801 Coffee Brown-dk.
Step 4: Beadwork		
	E	Robin's Egg Blue (MPR 143T)

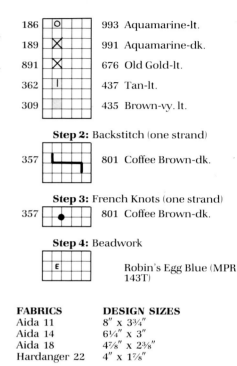

FABRICS	DESIGN SIZES
Aida 11	8″ x 3¾″
Aida 14	6¼″ x 3″
Aida 18	4⅞″ x 2⅜″
Hardanger 22	4″ x 1⅞″

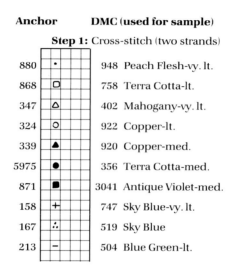

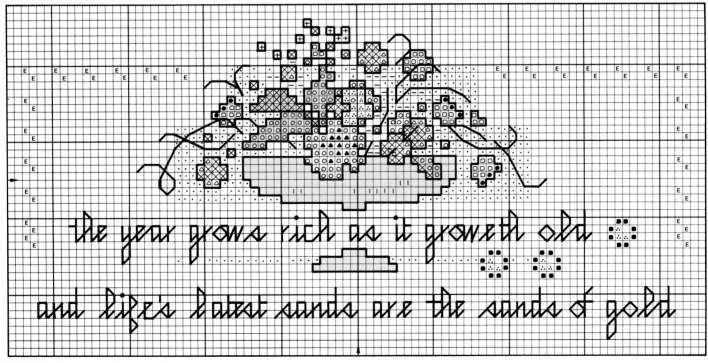

Stitch Count: 88 x 42

Merry Christmas!

SAMPLE

Stitched on white Linda 27 over two threads, the finished design size is 4¾" x 3⅞". (Adjust project measurements for other stitch counts.) The fabric was cut 8" x 8".

MATERIALS FOR CARD

Completed cross-stitch
One 10" x 16" piece of green print fabric; matching thread
1½ yards of ¹⁄₁₆"-wide blue rayon braid; matching thread
Fusible web
One 8" x 16" piece of medium-weight white paper
One 7¾" x 15" piece of light-weight paper
Rubber cement
Dressmakers' pen
Tracing paper

DIRECTIONS

1. Trace and cut out the heart pattern. Center the pattern over the stitched design and cut out. Cut one heart from the fusible web. Also cut one 10" x 15" piece of fusible web; set aside.

2. Place the Linda heart on the print fabric, centered horizontally 2" above one 10" edge. Fuse the heart to the print fabric, according to the manufacturer's directions.

3. Using green thread and widest stitch, machine-satin-stitch the edges of the heart. Cut two 22" lengths of braid. Tack one piece of braid to the heart, next to the satin-stitching. Leave 2½" ends loose at the bottom point of the heart. Repeat with the second piece of braid, tacking it parallel to and ⅛" inside the first piece. Fold the remaining braid in a 2" loop. Tie the braid ends around the center of the loop. Trim the ends.

4. Score the medium-weight paper in the center to make an 8" square card. Fold under ½" on both 10" edges of the print fabric; press. Center the fabric on the paper, leaving ½" of paper showing on each end and allowing for a small amount of "give" at the score line. Fuse the fabric to the card. Fold the excess fabric on the sides to the inside of the card and tack the edges down with glue.

5. Fold the lightweight paper to measure 7¾" x 7½". Place it inside the card, matching the fold line to the score line. Glue the paper along the score line and in the corners to hide the raw edges of the fabric.

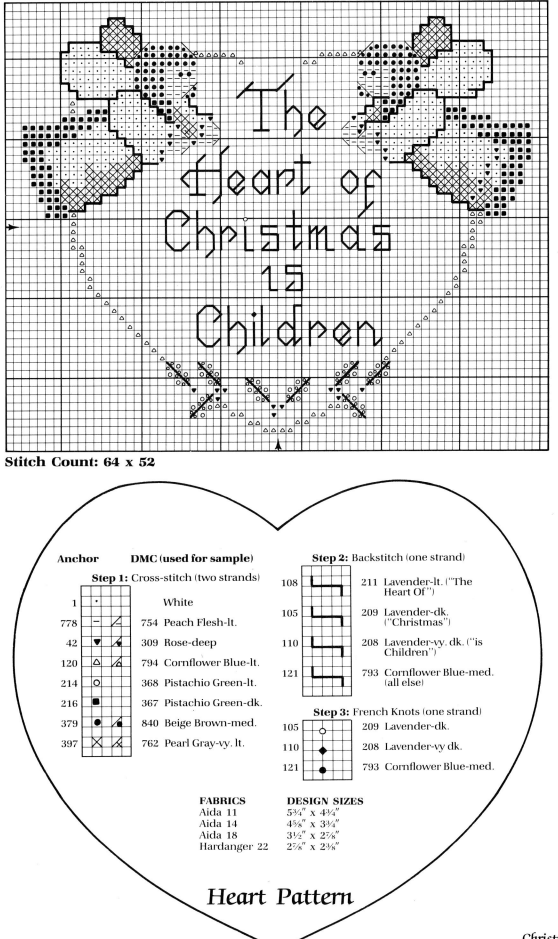

Stitch Count: 64 x 52

Anchor		DMC (used for sample)
	Step 1: Cross-stitch (two strands)	
1	·	White
778	− ╱	754 Peach Flesh-lt.
42	▼ ◣	309 Rose-deep
120	△ ◿	794 Cornflower Blue-lt.
214	○	368 Pistachio Green-lt.
216	■	367 Pistachio Green-dk.
379	● ◿	840 Beige Brown-med.
397	✕ ◿	762 Pearl Gray-vy. lt.

Step 2: Backstitch (one strand)

108		211 Lavender-lt. ("The Heart Of")
105		209 Lavender-dk. ("Christmas")
110		208 Lavender-vy. dk. ("is Children")
121		793 Cornflower Blue-med. (all else)

Step 3: French Knots (one strand)

105	○	209 Lavender-dk.
110	◆	208 Lavender-vy dk.
121	●	793 Cornflower Blue-med.

FABRICS	DESIGN SIZES
Aida 11	5¾" x 4¾"
Aida 14	4⅝" x 3¾"
Aida 18	3½" x 2⅞"
Hardanger 22	2⅞" x 2⅜"

Heart Pattern

*Wishing you
a joy-filled season*

Window Pattern

SAMPLE

Stitched on cream Belfast Linen 32 over two threads, the finished design size is 4⅞" x 5½". (Adjust project measurements for other stitch counts.) The fabric was cut 8" x 9".

MATERIALS FOR CARD

Completed cross-stitch
1¾ yards of ¹⁄₁₆"-wide purple rayon braid
Fusible web
One 7" x 16½" piece of medium-weight white paper
One 6¾" x 8" piece of watercolor paper
Green watercolor paint
Paintbrush
Rubber cement

Tracing paper
Craft knife with sharp blade

DIRECTIONS

1. Cut the linen 6¼" x 7", with the design centered. Cut the fusible web 6¼" x 7".

2. Trace and cut out the pattern for the window. On the back of the watercolor paper, center the pattern horizontally and 1" from the bottom edge. Trace and cut out the window to make the mat.

3. Paint the front of the mat with a thin wash of green paint. Be sure to coat the inside edge of the window as well.

4. Score the white paper in the center to make a 7" x 8¼" card.

5. With the design centered horizontally and 1¾" above the bottom edge of the card, fuse the linen to the front of the card.

6. Glue the painted mat to the front of the card.

7. Cut one 12" length of rayon braid. Fold the remaining braid into 3" loops. Tie the 12" length around the center of the loops. Glue the braid to the front of the card (see photo).

Stitch Count: 78 x 87

Anchor   DMC (used for sample)

Step 1: Cross-stitch (two strands)

876 | 502 Blue Green

Step 2: Backstitch

871 | 3041 Antique Violet-med. (one strand, lettering; two strands, all else)

Step 3: French Knots (one strand)

871 | 3041 Antique Violet-med.

Step 4: Beadwork

Light Green (MPR 525K)

FABRICS	DESIGN SIZES
Aida 11	7⅛″ x 7⅞″
Aida 14	5⅝″ x 6¼″
Aida 18	4⅜″ x 4⅞″
Hardanger 22	3½″ x 4″

MATERIALS FOR CARD

Completed cross-stitch
One 7″ x 5″ piece of polyester fleece
Six ⅜″ white buttons
One ⅝″ green button
8″ length of ⅛″-wide navy satin ribbon
One 7″ x 5″ piece of lightweight cardboard
One 7″ x 10″ piece of medium-weight tan paper
Glue
Transparent tape
Dressmakers' pen
Tracing paper

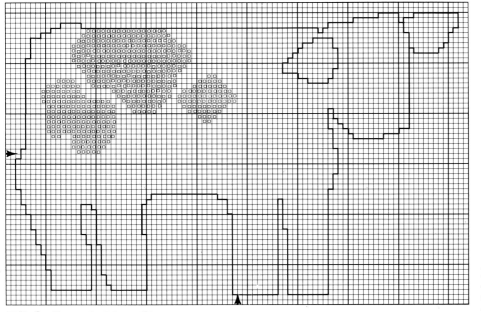

Happy Holidays!

SAMPLE

Stitched on white Aida 14, the finished design size is 6¼″ x 4″. (Adjust project measurements for other stitch counts.) The fabric was cut 11″ x 9″.

DIRECTIONS

1. Complete Steps 1–4 of the cow card on pages 54–55.

2. Glue the white buttons in place (see photo). Glue the green button below the white buttons. Tie the ribbon into a bow and glue near the first white button.

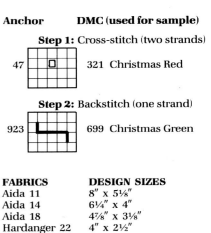

Anchor		DMC (used for sample)
	Step 1: Cross-stitch (two strands)	
47	▫	321 Christmas Red
	Step 2: Backstitch (one strand)	
923		699 Christmas Green

FABRICS	DESIGN SIZES
Aida 11	8″ x 5⅛″
Aida 14	6¼″ x 4″
Aida 18	4⅞″ x 3⅛″
Hardanger 22	4″ x 2½″

Stitch Count: 88 x 56

Stitched on white Aida 14, the finished design size is 7⅝" x 4⅞". (Adjust project measurements for other stitch counts.) The fabric was cut 18" x 12".

MATERIALS FOR COW

Completed cross-stitch
One 16" square of unstitched white Aida 14; matching thread

9 yards of 1/16"-wide green satin ribbon; matching thread
2 yards of ⅛"-wide green satin ribbon
½ yard of ⅛"-wide red satin ribbon
40 to 45 (½"-wide) red satin ribbon roses on wire stems
One 1"-wide brass bell
Large-eyed needle
Stuffing
4" wire hoop
¾ yard of lightweight wire
Florists' tape

Dressmakers' pen
Tracing paper

DIRECTIONS

All seam allowances are ¼".

1. Trace and cut out patterns on pages 58–59, adding ¼" seam allowances.

2. Center the pattern for the cow body over the stitched design and trace the outline with the dressmakers' pen. Mark the placement for the spots.

3. To make the spots, thread a 25" length of 1/16"-wide ribbon through the large-eyed needle. Following the outline of the spots, weave the ribbon through the Aida. To complete the vertical rows of ribbon, bring the needle up at the top of each spot and down at the bottom of the spot. Work your way across the spots, leaving two thread units of Aida between the rows of ribbon. Tack the ribbon ends to the wrong side of the Aida.

Diagram

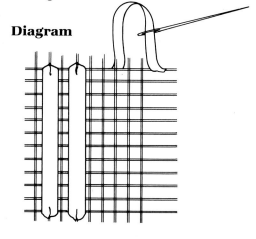

4. Complete the horizontal rows by weaving the ribbon over and

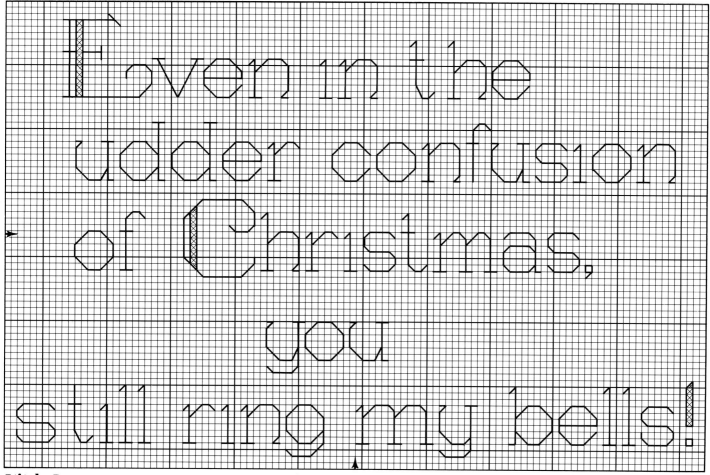

Stitch Count: 106 x 69

under the vertical rows. Tack the ribbon ends to the wrong side of the Aida.

5. Cut out the cow body from the stitched Aida. Cut one cow body and four ear pieces from the unstitched Aida.

6. Pin two ear pieces, right sides together and raw edges aligned. Stitch, leaving an opening for turning. Clip curves. Turn right side out and slipstitch the opening closed. Repeat for the second pair of ear pieces.

7. Pin the two body pieces, right sides together and raw edges aligned. Stitch, leaving an opening for turning. Clip curves. Turn right side out and stuff firmly. Slipstitch

the opening closed. To make the front legs, stitch through both layers along the stitching line on the right side of the cow. Backstitch to secure.

8. Tack the ears securely to the cow (see photo).

9. To make the cow's tail, cut four 8″ lengths of the ⅛″-wide green ribbon and two 8″ lengths of the red ribbon. Knot all lengths together and braid, using three units of two ribbons each. Tack the tail to the body. Knot the tail 5″ from the body. Trim the ribbon ends.

10. To make the cow's garland, wrap the wire hoop with florists' tape. Place the ribbon roses close together, wrapping the wire stems

around the hoop. Fold 1″ loops in the remaining ⅛″-wide green ribbon and, without cutting the ribbon, secure loops to hoop by wrapping the wire through the ribbon roses. Attach the bell and place the garland around the cow's neck.

Anchor		DMC (used for sample)	
Step 1: Cross-stitch (two strands)			
229		700	Christmas Green-bright
Step 2: Backstitch (one strand)			
229		700	Christmas Green-bright

FABRICS	DESIGN SIZES
Aida 11	9⅝″ x 6¼″
Aida 18	5⅞″ x 3⅞″
Hardanger 22	4⅞″ x 3⅛″

"The Twelve Days of Christmas"

On the first day of Christmas
You thought it was a partridge in a pear tree
But when you looked again
It was just a gift from me!

On the second day of Christmas
I saw two turtle doves
Toasting one another
And cooing about love!

On the third day of Christmas
I was joined by three French hens
Wishing you a pleasant evening
When you take a movie in!

On the fourth day of Christmas
Hear four calling birds
Who say, "Eat all of those cookies!"
And that's the final word.

On the fifth day of Christmas
Five golden rings are brought
As a special holiday gift
Which I hope you like a lot!

On the sixth day of Christmas
Before your very eyes
These six geese are bringing you
A wonderful surprise!

On the seventh day of Christmas
Seven swans went swimming past
They were in such a hurry…
Please open this present fast!

On the eighth day of Christmas
Those eight maids looked so silly~
Instead of pails of milk
It was great big bowls of chili!

On the ninth day of Christmas
Nine ladies were so-o-oo shy
But holiday spirits made them smile
As they went dancing by!

On the tenth day of Christmas
Those ten leapin' lords were ready
For an Italian celebration
Of specially made spaghetti!

On the eleventh day of Christmas
Eleven pipers play a tune
And hope this gift of love
Causes joy to fill the room!

On the twelfth day of Christmas
Twelve drummers made a fuss…
To finally let you know
These gifts have come from us!

MATERIALS FOR ONE TAG

Completed cross-stitch; matching thread
One small piece of unstitched Aida
One small piece of medium-weight white paper
Dressmakers' pen
Fifth Day Tag:
    Five gold rings
Ninth Day Tag:
    2½ yards of ¹⁄₁₆"-wide light blue satin ribbon; matching thread
Eleventh Day Tag:
    ⅝ yard of ¹⁄₁₆"-wide red rayon braid
    Three ½" red buttons
Twelfth Day Tag:
    1¼ yards of ¹⁄₁₆"-wide red rayon braid

DIRECTIONS

All seam allowances are ¼".

1. Measure the stitched design. To make a pattern for the tag, measure and cut the paper so that it is ½" to ¾" larger than the top, bottom, and one side edge of the design. Cut the remaining side edge 2½" to 3" larger than the design; mark the center of this edge and cut a point.

2. Position the paper tag over the design and, with the dressmakers' pen, trace around it onto the design piece. Add a ¼" seam allowance, except on the point. Pin the design piece to the unstitched Aida, right sides together and raw edges aligned. Stitch around the tag, leaving the point of the tag open for turning. Clip the corners

and turn right side out. Insert the paper tag.

3. Machine-satin-stitch the edge of the point through all layers. Topstitch ⅛" inside all edges.

4. For the following tags, complete these specific instructions:

Fifth Day Tag: Tack the gold rings to the tag (see photo).
Ninth Day Tag: Cut one 45" length of ribbon. Curl the ribbon by pulling it across the blade of a pair of scissors. Drape the ribbon around the edges of the tag, beginning and ending at the lower right corner. Tack the ribbon to the tag front at ¾"–1" intervals. Cut a 2" piece of ribbon from the remaining 45" length and set aside. Form 3" loops with the long piece of ribbon. Knot the 2" length around the center of the loops. Tack or glue the bow near the point.
Eleventh Day Tag: Cut three 1" lengths of braid. Slipstitch all lengths to the upper right corner of the tag, angling them down ¼" at the top (see photo). Sew a button over the lower end of each braid piece. Knot one end of the remaining braid. Beginning at the lower left corner of the tag, shape a treble clef (see photo). Knot the second end. Tack or glue treble clef to the tag.
Twelfth Day Tag: Cut a 12" length of braid. Glue the braid ¼" inside and parallel to the edges of the tag. Cut a 3" length of braid; set aside. Fold the remaining braid into 2" loops. Knot the 3" length around the center of the loops. Tack or glue the bow to the pointed end of the tag.

SAMPLE (1st day)

Stitched on white Aida 14, the finished design size is 2¾" x 2¾". (Adjust project measurements for other stitch counts.) The fabric was cut 10" x 6".

Anchor		DMC (used for sample)
Step 1: Cross-stitch (two strands)		
1	·	White
886	o	677 Old Gold-vy. lt.
891	X	676 Old Gold-lt.
778	−	754 Peach Flesh-lt.
969	▯	316 Antique Mauve-med.
970	∴	315 Antique Mauve-dk.
22	●	814 Garnet-dk.
159	■	827 Blue-vy. lt.
214	+	368 Pistachio Green-lt.
876	△	502 Blue Green
879	▲	500 Blue Green-vy. dk.

	Step 2: Backstitch (one strand)	
22		814 Garnet-dk.

FABRICS	DESIGN SIZES
Aida 11	3½" x 3½"
Aida 18	2⅛" x 2⅛"
Hardanger 22	1¾" x 1¾"

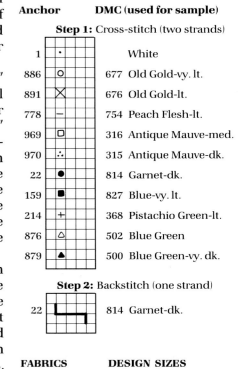

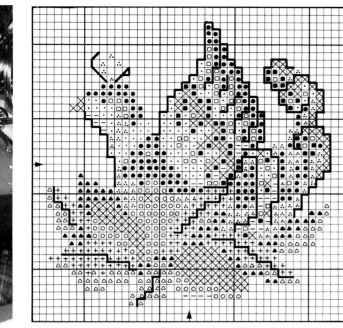

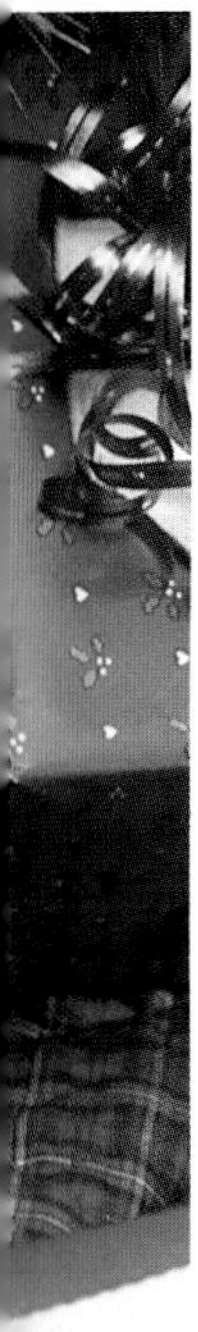

Stitch Count (1st day): 38 x 38

SAMPLE (2nd day)

Stitched on white Aida 14, the finished design size is 4⅝" x 2⅜". (Adjust project measurements for other stitch counts.) The fabric was cut 11" x 6".

Anchor			DMC (used for sample)
Step 1: Cross-stitch (two strands)			
1	·	╱	White
887	−	╱	3046 Yellow Beige-med.
59	●	▲	600 Cranberry-vy. dk.
130	○	╱	809 Delft
397	✕	╱	762 Pearl Gray-vy. lt.
Step 2: Backstitch (one strand)			
131			798 Delft.-dk. (ribbon)
401			413 Pewter Gray-dk. (eyes)
400			414 Steel Gray-dk. (all else)

FABRICS	DESIGN SIZES
Aida 11	5¾" x 3"
Aida 18	3½" x 1⅞"
Hardanger 22	2⅞" x 1½"

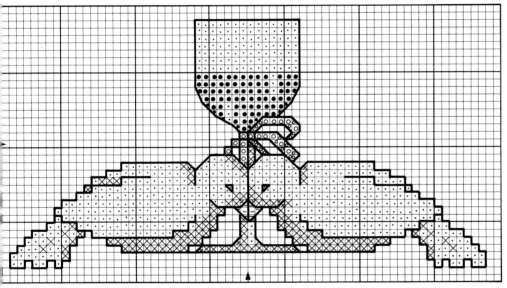

titch Count (2nd day): 64 x 33

SAMPLE (3rd day)

Stitched on white Aida 14, the finished design size is 1½" x 1¾". (Adjust project measurements for other stitch counts.) The fabric was cut 8" x 5".

Anchor		DMC (used for sample)
Step 1: Cross-stitch (two strands)		
206	·	955 Nile Green-lt.
203	−	954 Nile Green
209	○	913 Nile Green-med.
204	+	912 Emerald Green-lt.
205	∴	911 Emerald Green-med.
228	✕	910 Emerald Green-dk.
229	■	909 Emerald Green-vy. dk.

FABRICS	DESIGN SIZES
Aida 11	1⅞" x 2¼"
Aida 18	1⅛" x 1⅜"
Hardanger 22	1" x 1⅛"

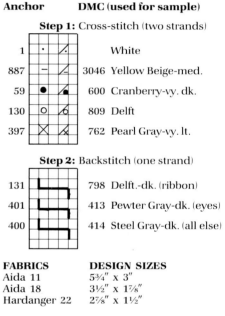

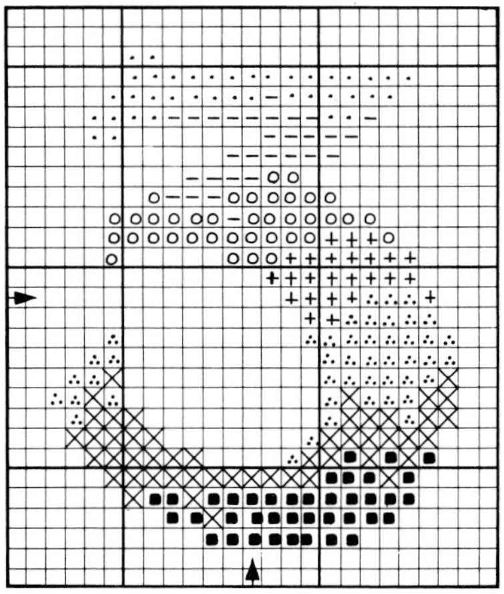

Stitch Count (3rd day): 21 x 25

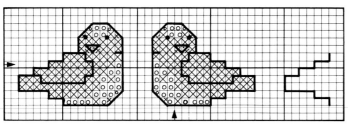

Stitch Count (4th day): 32 x 11 (two birds)

SAMPLE (4th day)

Stitched on white Aida 14, the finished design size is 2¼" x ¾". (Adjust project measurements for other stitch counts.) The fabric was cut 11" x 4".

Anchor			DMC (used for sample)

Step 1: Cross-stitch (two strands)

128			800 Delft-pale
130			799 Delft-med.
403			310 Black

Step 2: Backstitch (one strand)

| 403 | | 310 Black |

Step 3: French Knots (one strand)

| 403 | | 310 Black |

FABRICS	DESIGN SIZES
Aida 11	2⅞" x 1"
Aida 18	1¾" x ⅝"
Hardanger 22	1½" x ½"

SAMPLE (6th day)

Stitched on white Aida 14, the finished design size is 4¾" x 3⅛". (Adjust project measurements for other stitch counts.) The fabric was cut 11" x 6".

Anchor			DMC (used for sample)

Step 1: Cross-stitch (two strands)

1			White
316			740 Tangerine
205			911 Emerald Green-med.
397			762 Pearl Gray-vy. lt.

Step 2: Backstitch (one strand)

46		666 Christmas Red-bright (ribbons on wreathed geese)
89		915 Plum-dk. (ribbons on unwreathed geese)
400		414 Steel Gray-dk. (geese)

SAMPLE (5th day)

Stitched on white Aida 14, the finished design size is 2¼" x 2¼". (Adjust project measurements for other stitch counts.) The fabric was cut 10" x 7".

Anchor		DMC (used for sample)

Step 1: Backstitch (one strand)

| 229 | | 909 Emerald Green-vy. dk. |

FABRICS	DESIGN SIZES
Aida 11	3" x 3"
Aida 18	1¾" x 1¾"
Hardanger 22	1½" x 1½"

134 *Christmas*

Stitch Count (5th day): 32 x 32

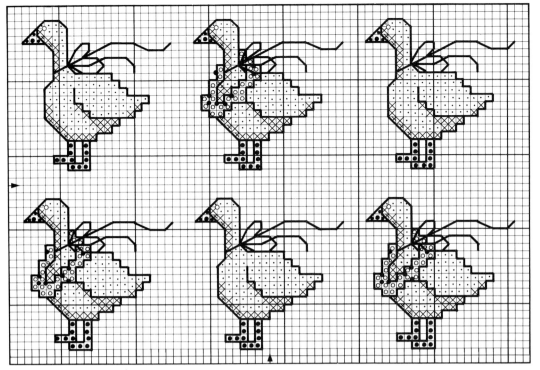

Stitch Count (6th day): 66 x 44

Step 3: French Knots (one strand)

46	666 Christmas Red-bright
400	414 Steel Gray-dk.

FABRICS **DESIGN SIZES**
Aida 11   6″ x 4″
Aida 18   3⅝″ x 2½″
Hardanger 22   3″ x 2″

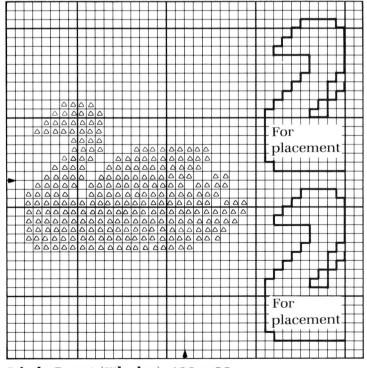

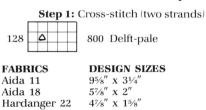

For placement

For placement

SAMPLE (7th day)

Stitched on white Aida 14, the finished design size is 7⅝″ x 2⅝″. (Adjust project measurements for other stitch counts.) The fabric was cut 15″ x 8″. Stitch seven swans, two stitches apart; see graph for placement.

Anchor   **DMC (used for sample)**

Step 1: Cross-stitch (two strands)

128	800 Delft-pale

FABRICS **DESIGN SIZES**
Aida 11   9⅝″ x 3¼″
Aida 18   5⅞″ x 2″
Hardanger 22   4⅞″ x 1⅝″

Stitch Count (7th day): 106 x 36

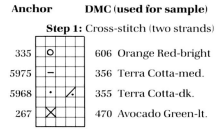
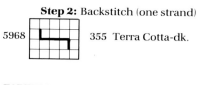
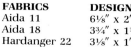

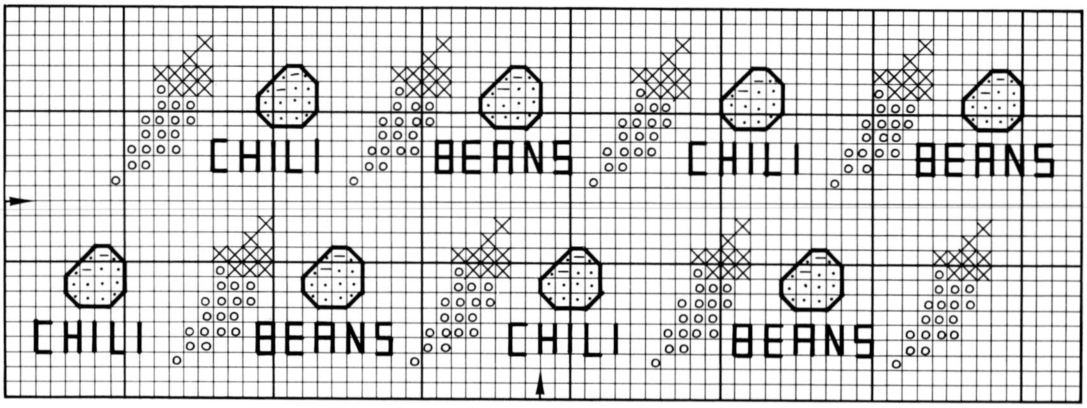

Stitch Count (8th day): 68 x 22

SAMPLE (8th day)

Stitched on white Aida 14, the finished design size is 4⅞″ x 1⅝″. (Adjust project measurements for other stitch counts.) The fabric was cut 10″ x 5″.

Anchor		DMC (used for sample)	
		Step 1: Cross-stitch (two strands)	
335	O	606	Orange Red-bright
5975	–	356	Terra Cotta-med.
5968	· /	355	Terra Cotta-dk.
267	X	470	Avocado Green-lt.

		Step 2: Backstitch (one strand)	
5968		355	Terra Cotta-dk.

FABRICS	DESIGN SIZES
Aida 11	6⅛″ x 2″
Aida 18	3¾″ x 1¼″
Hardanger 22	3⅛″ x 1″

SAMPLE (9th day)

Stitched on white Aida 14, the finished design size is 3⅜″ x 1⅝″. (Adjust project measurements for other stitch counts.) The fabric was cut 10″ x 7″.

Anchor		DMC (used for sample)	
		Step 1: Cross-stitch (two strands)	
26	·	3708	Melon-lt.
28	–	3706	Melon-med.
35	O	3705	Melon-dk.

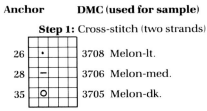

		Step 2: Backstitch (one strand)	
59		326	Rose-vy. deep

		Step 3: Long Stitch (two strands)	
131		798	Delft-dk.
88		718	Plum
26		3708	Melon-lt.

Step 4: Beadwork

∴	Yellow (MPR 128T)
X	Tangerine (MPR 423)
■	Red (MPR 968K)
△	Iris (MPR 252T)

FABRICS	DESIGN SIZES
Aida 11	4¼″ x 2″
Aida 18	2⅝″ x 1¼″
Hardanger 22	2⅛″ x 1″

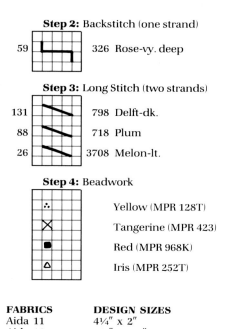

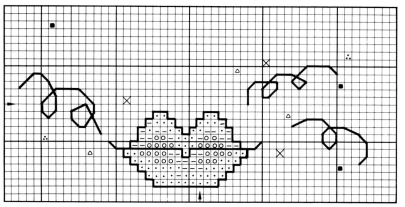

Stitch Count (9th day): 47 x 22

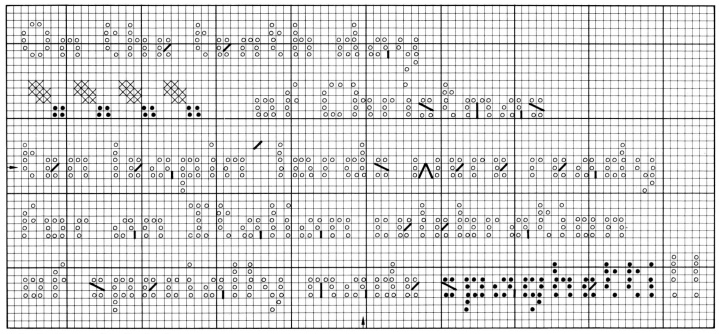

Stitch Count (10th day): 91 x 39

SAMPLE (10th day)

Stitched on white Aida 14, the finished design size is 6½″ x 2¾″. (Adjust project measurements for other stitch counts.) The fabric was cut 14″ x 8″.

Anchor		DMC (used for sample)

Step 1: Cross-stitch (two strands)

Anchor		DMC	
19	●	817	Coral Red-vy. dk.
239	O	702	Kelly Green
229	X	700	Christmas Green-bright

Step 2: Backstitch (one strand)

Anchor		DMC	
19		817	Coral Red-vy. dk. ('spaghetti')
239		702	Kelly Green (all else)

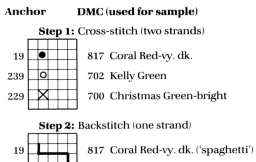

FABRICS	DESIGN SIZES
Aida 11	8¼″ x 3½″
Aida 18	5″ x 2⅛″
Hardanger 22	4⅛″ x 1¾″

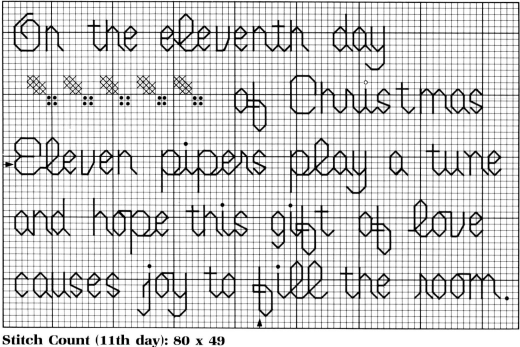

Stitch Count (11th day): 80 x 49

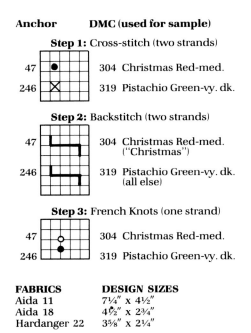

SAMPLE (11th day)

Stitched on white Aida 14, the finished design size is 5¾" x 3½". (Adjust project measurements for other stitch counts.) The fabric was cut 16" x 10".

Anchor		DMC (used for sample)
Step 1: Cross-stitch (two strands)		
47	●	304 Christmas Red-med.
246	✕	319 Pistachio Green-vy. dk.

		Step 2: Backstitch (two strands)
47		304 Christmas Red-med. ("Christmas")
246		319 Pistachio Green-vy. dk. (all else)

		Step 3: French Knots (one strand)
47	○	304 Christmas Red-med.
246	●	319 Pistachio Green-vy. dk.

FABRICS	DESIGN SIZES
Aida 11	7¼" x 4½"
Aida 18	4½" x 2¾"
Hardanger 22	3⅝" x 2¼"

SAMPLE (12th day)

Stitched on white Aida 14, the finished design size is 3¼" x 1". (Adjust project measurements for other stitch counts.) The fabric was cut 12" x 4".

Anchor		DMC (used for sample)
Step 1: Cross-stitch (two strands)		
891	▲	676 Old Gold-lt.
46	○ ⟋	666 Christmas Red-bright
978		322 Navy Blue-vy. lt.
239	✕ ⟍	702 Kelly Green
	□	Silver Metallic

		Step 2: Backstitch (one strand)
149		311 Navy Blue-med.

		Step 3: Long Stitch
149		311 Navy Blue-med. (two strands, drum handle)
		Gold Metallic (one strand, drum laces)

		Step 4: French Knots (one strand)
149	● ○	Gold Metallic
		311 Navy Blue-med.

FABRICS	DESIGN SIZES
Aida 11	4⅛" x 1¼"
Aida 18	2½" x ¾"
Hardanger 22	2⅛" x ⅝"

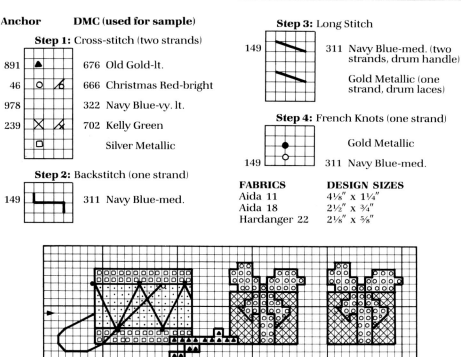

Stitch Count (12th day): 46 x 14

General Instructions

Cross-Stitch

1. Zigzag the edges of the fabric.

2. Cut the floss into 18″ lengths. Dampen and separate the strands. Put together the number needed.

3. Locate the center of the design on the graph by following the vertical and horizontal arrows. Then locate the center of the fabric.

4. Before you begin stitching, make a waste knot. Knot the floss and insert your needle in the fabric front, 1″ from the center. Bring the needle up at center of fabric and begin stitching (Diagram A). Work several stitches over thread to secure; then cut the knot.

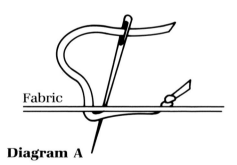

Diagram A

5. Make one cross for each symbol (Diagram B). For rows, stitch first half of cross from left to right; then fill in second half of cross from right to left (Diagram C). Stitches should lie in the same direction.

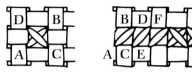

Diagram B   **Diagram C**

6. Filet cross-stitch is simply cross-stitch that uses only one strand of embroidery floss.

7. For half-crosses, make the longer stitch in the direction of the slanted line (Diagram D).

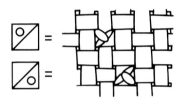

Diagram D

8. Backstitching is used to outline and accent (Diagram E). Use one strand less than for cross-stitch unless otherwise specified.

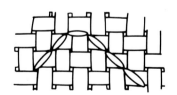

Diagram E

9. When stitching on paper, follow pattern carefully so stitches will not have to be pulled out. If stitches are removed, unsightly holes will remain in the paper.

Cards

Paper: In this book, "lightweight" paper means watercolor paper (or a similar weight), "medium-weight" means poster board, and "heavyweight" means mat board.

Score Line: A score line is a mark or shallow cut made with the blade of a knife into, but not through, a surface. (Scoring will make folding stiff paper easier.)

Marking and Cutting Windows: Find the center of the square or rectangle of paper by drawing a diagonal line from one corner of the paper to the opposite corner. Repeat for other two corners. The center is the point at which lines intersect.

Measure between the diagonal lines and mark the specified dimensions. Make sure the edges of the window are parallel to the outside edges of the paper. Place a straightedge on the window lines and cut with a craft knife.

To cut a shaped window, transfer the pattern to the back of the paper. Instead of moving the craft knife along the lines of the pattern, hold the knife still and move the *paper*.

Glue: The instructions in this book use the word "glue" to indicate a process using two products: rubber cement to bond paper to paper or white glue to bond beads, buttons, ribbons, and some fabric pieces to paper. In some cases, fusing material is used to bond fabric to paper.

Envelopes

Envelope Size

Envelope Size: To make an envelope to fit a card in this book, add ½″ to both the length and the width of the card to determine the desired size of the envelope when closed. Adjust the pattern to make all the remaining envelope measurements proportional to these dimensions.

1. DIAPER-FOLD ENVELOPE

Materials

One 18″ square of print fabric
One 18″ square of plain fabric
¼ yard of 45″-wide contrasting print fabric; matching thread
Two ½″ buttons
Fusible web
Tracing paper

Directions

1. Make the pattern for the envelope (Diagram A). Trace the pattern onto the print fabric. Fuse the lining to the wrong side of the print fabric. Cut out the envelope.

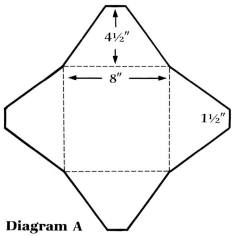

Diagram A

2. Cut a 1¼″-wide bias strip from the contrasting print fabric, piecing as needed to equal 1¾ yards. Stitch right sides of binding and lining together on all sides with a ¼″ seam. Fold the binding double to the right side of the envelope. Topstitch close to the folded edge, mitering binding at the corners.

3. Fold three flaps toward center of envelope. Sew the buttons through all three flaps. On the top flap, make buttonholes to match (Diagram B). Button the envelope closed.

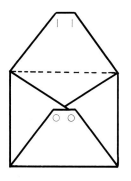

Diagram B

2. DRAWSTRING FABRIC ENVELOPE

Materials

One 10½" x 9¼" piece of print fabric; matching thread
1¼ yards of ½"-wide variegated silk ribbon
Seam ripper

·Directions

1. Cut one 10½" length of ribbon. Sew the ribbon to the right side of the print fabric, 1¾" above one 10½" edge of the fabric; stitch along both edges of the ribbon.

2. Fold the print fabric with right sides together to measure 5¼" x 9¼". Stitch the side and bottom to make a bag. Clip the corners and turn right side out.

3. To make the casing, fold ¼" and then ½" to the wrong side along the top edge. Stitch ½" from the top edge through all layers.

4. Use a seam ripper to carefully cut the threads in the side seam between the stitching line and the top of the bag. Thread the ribbon through the casing. Tie a knot in each ribbon end.

3. TOP-FOLDED FABRIC ENVELOPE

Materials

One 14" x 12" piece of print fabric; matching thread

¾ yard of ⅛"-wide satin ribbon; matching thread

Directions

1. Fold the fabric with right sides together to measure 7" x 12". Stitch the side and bottom to make a bag. Clip the corners and turn right side out.

2. Fold ¼" double to the wrong side at the top of the bag. Stitch the hem.

3. Flatten the bag and fold the top 1½" to the front. Fold top 1½" again. Mark the fold and the bag for ribbon placement.

4. Cut the ribbon into four equal lengths. Tack the ribbons to the marks. Fold the top over and tie the ribbons into bows to close the envelope.

4. LINEN ENVELOPE

Materials

¼ yard of 55"-wide white Belfast Linen 32; matching thread
¼ yard of ⅛"-wide white satin ribbon
Four ½" white/gold heart buttons
Tracing paper

Directions

1. Make the pattern for the flap (Diagram C). Cut two 7½" x 12" and two 7½" x 9¼" pieces of linen. Stack the two 7½" x 12" pieces of fabric. Trace the flap pattern onto the fabric with the curved edge at one 7½" end. Cut around the curved edge only, through both layers.

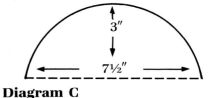

Diagram C

2. Match the bottom edge of one small linen piece to the bottom edge of one large piece with the right sides together. Stitch the sides only. Repeat for the remaining pieces of linen.

3. Turn one unit right side out. Slide that unit inside the other so that right sides are together and side seams are matched. Stitch around the entire top edge. Clip the curved seam allowance. Turn right side out and tuck one unit inside the other for lining.

4. Fold the bottom edge of the envelope (all layers) up ¼". Then fold up edge 1" and tuck corners in (Diagram D). Slipstitch to one layer only.

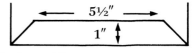

Diagram D

5. Fold the ribbon in half. Tack the fold of the ribbon 1" from the center of the flap edge. Sew the button over the ribbon fold. Fold down the envelope flap. Sew a second button 1½" below the first button. Thread each ribbon end through the shank of a remaining button. Knot the ribbon ends to secure the buttons.

5. WRAPPING PAPER ENVELOPE

Materials

One 8″ x 11″ piece of heavy
 wrapping paper
Rubber cement
Tracing paper

Directions

1. Make the pattern for the envelope (Diagram E). Trace the pattern onto the wrong side of the paper and cut out.

Diagram E   Side

2. Fold in the sides of the envelope. Fold the top and bottom. Glue the bottom flap to side tabs. Trim the top flap to the desired depth.

6. FELT ENVELOPE

Materials

One 8″ x 17″ piece of cream felt;
 matching thread
One 8″ x 12″ piece of pink felt
Embroidery scissors
Tracing paper

Directions

1. Trace and cut out the patterns, one for the cream felt and one for the pink felt.

2. Pin the pattern for the cream flap with the rounded edge to one 8″ edge of the cream felt. Cutting through the paper and the felt, cut around the outside edge and cut out the filigree pattern.

3. Pin the lining pattern to one 8″ edge of the pink felt; cut around the outside edge only.

4. Place the pink felt behind the cream felt so that the pink flap edge extends ¼″ beyond the cream flap edge. Trim both pieces even on the opposite 8″ edge. Fold cream felt up at the bottom edge of the pink felt to make a pocket. Pin.

5. With the cream side of envelope up, stitch the cream felt to the pink felt just inside the edge of the cream felt. Trim the sides close to the stitching.

Pink Lining Pattern

Cream Flap Pattern

7. SCALLOPED PAPER ENVELOPE

Materials

One 7¾" x 5½" piece of
medium-weight paper;
matching thread
1 yard of ¹⁄₁₆"-wide satin ribbon
Rubber cement
Tracing paper

Directions

1. Make the pattern for the envelope (Diagram F). Trace and cut the envelope out of paper. Fold in the 1" side and then the 3¼" side. Glue.

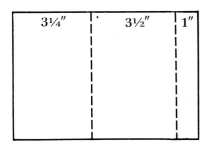

Diagram F

2. Stitch across the bottom, ¾" from the edge. Draw ½" to ⅝"-wide scallops, equally distributed across the bottom of the envelope. Cut scallops through all layers.

3. Make a small hole through all layers, ¼" from the top edge and ¾" from one side of the envelope. Repeat for other side. Cut the ribbon in half. Thread a ribbon length through each hole and tie bows to close the envelope.

8. LARGE PAPER ENVELOPE

Materials

One 14" x 10" piece of medium-weight paper
¾ yard of ⅛"-wide satin ribbon
Rubber cement
Small piece of cardboard
Craft knife
Tracing paper

Directions

1. Make the pattern for the envelope (Diagram G). Trace the pattern onto the wrong side of the paper and cut out.

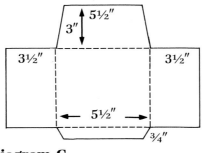

Diagram G

2. Fold in the sides of the envelope and glue. Fold up the bottom and glue. Fold down the top flap.

3. Insert the cardboard to protect the envelope front. Make two ¼" slits 1" on either side of the center back, cutting through the top flap and the back only. Remove cardboard. Thread the ribbon through slits in the back and flap. Tie a bow to close the envelope.

Suppliers

All products are available retail from Shepherd's Bush, 220 24th Street, Ogden, UT 84401; (801)399-4546; or for a merchant near you, write the following suppliers:

Zweigart Fabrics—Zweigart®/Joan Toggitt Ltd., 35 Fairfield Place, West Caldwell, NJ 07006
Zweigart Fabrics used:

White Aida 18	White Linda 27
White Aida 14	Toffee Oslo 22
White Aida 11	Waste Canvas 14
Cream Aida 18	Yellow Aida 18
Cream Aida 14	Black Aida 18
Light Blue Aida 14	
Brown Aida 14	
Cream Hardanger 22	
White Belfast Linen 32	
Cream Belfast Linen 32	
Driftwood Belfast Linen 32	

Other fabrics used include:

Fiddlers Cloth 14—Charles Craft, P.O. Box 1049, Laurinburg, NC 28352.

Glenshee Egyptian Cotton Quality O and Gray Glenshee Linen 29—Anne Powell Heirloom Stitchery, P.O. Box 3060, Stuart, FL 33495.

Linen Plus 28—Craft World, P.O. Box 779, New Windsor, MD 21776.

Natural Linen Plus 28—Regency Mills, 251 Grant Avenue, Building 39, 2nd Floor, East Newark, NJ 07029.

Canvas Tiny Totes—Chapelle Designers, P.O. Box 9252, Newgate Station, Ogden, UT 84409.

Perforated Paper—Astor Place, 239 Main Avenue, Stirling, NJ 07980.

Beads—MPR Associates, P.O. Box 7343, High Point, NC 27264.

Ribbon—C.M. Offray & Son, Route 24, Box 601, Chester, NJ 07930-0601.

Buttons—The Hands Work, P.O. Box 386, Pecos, NM 87552.

The Vanessa-Ann Collection Staff

Owners:
Terrece Beesley Woodruff
and Jo Packham

Executive Editor:
Margaret Shields Marti

Editor:
Monica Smith

Art Director:
Trice Liljenquist Boerens

Needlework Director:
Nancy Whitley

Graphic Artist:
Julie Truman

Graphing Director:
Susan Jorgensen

Operations Director:
Pamela Randall

Administrative Assistant:
Barbara Milburn

Customer Relations:
Kathi Allred

Designers

Trice Boerens	Vickie Everhart	Julie Truman
Linda Durbano	Margaret Marti	Terrece Woodruff
	Jo Packham	